The House of Self

Note from the Author

In 1981 I assumed the name Mariamne Paulus to express my commitment to take my place publicly as a Light Bearer and as a Wisdom teacher. All books written before the year 2001 carried my given and married names. This series on the Wisdom Teachings, however, is published under the name that carries the frequency of the Wisdom Tradition and that I use in my teaching.

Books by Diane Kennedy Pike

As Mariamne Paulus:
Awakening to Wisdom

Four Paths to Union

As Diane Kennedy Pike:
Life As A Waking Dream

The Love Project Way (with Arleen Lorrance)

My Journey Into Self: Phase One

Life Is Victorious!
How to Grow Through Grief

Cosmic Unfoldment

Channeling Love Energy (with Arleen Lorrance)

The Wilderness Revolt (with R. Scott Kennedy)

Search

As Diane Kennedy:
The Other Side (with James A. Pike)

The House Of Self

A Description of the Structure and Function of the Individual's Energy Field

By MARIAMNE PAULUS

Teleos Imprint ~ Scottsdale, AZ

Teleos Imprint
Wisdom Books
Published by LP Publications
7119 E Shea Blvd.
Suite 109 PMB 418
Scottsdale, AZ 85254-6107

Copyright 2005 by Diane Kennedy Pike
All rights reserved.

The Teleos Institute World Wide Web site address is
http://www.teleosinstitute.com

    Library of Congress Cataloging-in-Publication Data

Pike, Diane Kennedy.
  The house of self : a description of the structure and function of the individual's energy field / by Mariamne Paulus.-- 1st ed.
    p. cm.
  Includes bibliographical references.
  ISBN 0-916192-49-0 (pbk. : alk. paper)
 1. Self-actualization (Psychology)--Miscellanea. 2. Consciousness--Miscellanea. 3. Chakras--Miscellanea. I. Title.
BF1999.P5493 2006
131--dc22
                        2005030830

First Printing, 2006
Printed in the United States of America

Photo on front cover by **Arleen Lorrance**

Teleos Imprint
Cascade of Angels

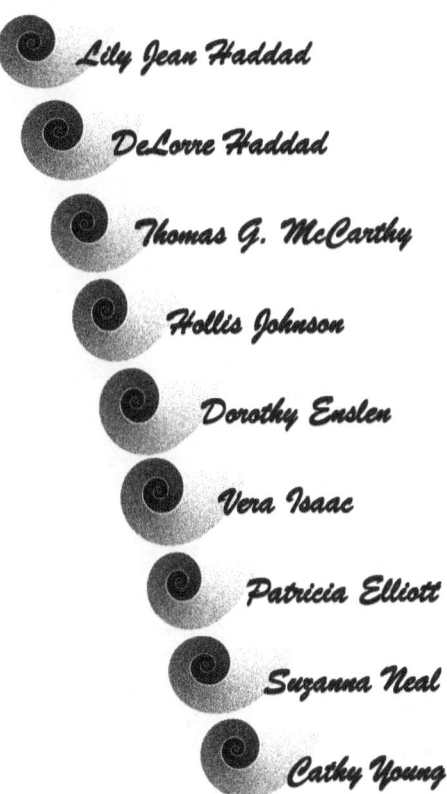

- Lily Jean Haddad
- DeLorre Haddad
- Thomas G. McCarthy
- Hollis Johnson
- Dorothy Enslen
- Vera Isaac
- Patricia Elliott
- Suzanna Neal
- Cathy Young

Would you like to be included in our cascade of angels?
Call 480-471-3082 or e-mail ljh4848@aol.com

Words of Gratitude

My thanks to the members of the 2004 Energy Odyssey for their feedback and encouragement as they read this book in rough manuscript form. It was a special challenge for me to write a book for their study, with the intent of releasing it in published form at a later date, and they helped me feel at ease with the process.

Thanks to Patricia Nerison for her careful reading and editing of the final manuscript. Her suggestions brought polish to the text that would have been lacking without her expertise.

Thanks also to Pamela Reily and Patricia Nerison for proof-reading the text before it went to press.

To my partner Arleen Lorrance go my thanks for all her encouragement as well as for her suggestions for the improvement of the text, which she read several times on its way to completion. Arleen is my companion in the teaching of the Wisdom and I value her perceptions enormously.

Thanks also to the Angels who are named on a previous page, and most especially to Lily Jean Haddad. Their financial contributions, and Lily Jean's efforts in raising the money, have made possible the publishing of the *Teleos Imprint Wisdom Book* series.

I dedicate this book to the

2004 Energy Odyssey Participants

Eleanor Arnau, Sarah Beynon, Margarite Bradley,
Katharina Bruner, Sandy Coyne, Andy Gould,
Lily Jean Haddad, Carol Kearney, Tom McCarthy,
Maureen McCready, Suzanna Neal, Patricia Nerison,
Anita Pitcher, Maggie Reid, Dallas Sweig,
and Cathy Young

Their spirit of adventure as they explored the energy world and the structure of their energetic Houses of Self provided me with both inspiration and companionship.

Contents

Introduction i
Words about Esoteric Astrology iii
1. The House of Self 3
2. Force and Form 25
3. The Creative Force 49
4. Freedom to Direct Forces 61
5. Learning How to Feel 77
6. From Water to Air 99
7. Drying Out 119
8. Figuring It All Out 145
9. Reflecting the Light 165
10. Reorienting Ourselves: From Outer to Inner 185
11. From Air to Fire 203
12. The Work of Regeneration 227
Quick Guide to Practice Exercises 241
Bibliography 243

Illustrations

#1. Fields Within Fields 10
#2. The House of Self 15
#3. Nested Energy Bands (before awakening) 18
#4. Nested Energy Bands (after awakening) 19
#5. The Body as an Energy Pattern 27
#6. The Seven Rays 32
#7. The Seven Chakras 33
#8. The Seven Rays Motivating Humans
    through the Seven Chakras 43
#9. The Caduceus 71
#10. The Elements and the Chakras 133
#11. The Autonomous Field: The House of Self 205
#12. Astrological Symbols and the Chakras 239

Introduction

The following is intended as an instructional guide for individuals who have begun the awakening process. I mean those in particular who have begun to cooperate consciously with the transformation occurring in their consciousness, a change that causes people to break away from identification with groups and to build the courage to stand alone and confident in their own knowing. Eventually these individuals will be so whole and complete in themselves that they will know, simultaneously, their uniqueness and their oneness with All that Is and All who Are.

When I refer to the awakening process, I mean that time period in our lives when we begin to ask the fundamental questions in life: Who am I? Why am I here? What is the nature of life? Is there death? What is real? When a profound longing *to know through our own experience* accompanies wrestling with such questions, then we have begun to awaken. We have joined a large company of individuals who, through the ages, have made just this response to the pressure from within to become who we are destined to become: conscious centers of expression of the One Self.

One way of describing the process of awakening is to say that it is learning to function in the energy world, that is, the dynamic reality "behind" our objective images of what is. This book is an attempt to provide words, concepts, and images for individuals who are being thrust by the life force[1] into such functioning. I hope that it will hasten their reorientation and make their way easier.

I am indebted to my teacher Vitvan[2] for the metaphor of the House of Self, though I have elaborated considerably on his presentation of it. I am also indebted to Vitvan and to the philosophy of yoga for much of my understanding of the chakra system.

The bulk of what I offer represents the harvest of my own process of awakening up to this point. I am well acquainted with the lunar phase of the unfolding process (see pages 68ff below), having been deep into it for most of this lifetime, and I have had glimpses of the solar phase (see Chapters Eleven and Twelve). I have drawn on the reports of those farther along the path for what I lack in personal experience.

My purpose has been to make a faithful verbal representation of the energetic structure of the individual and of the function of each of the chakras both before and during the process of awakening. It is my hope that this will serve others as guideposts on their own journeys.

— *Mariamne Paulus*
a.k.a. Diane Kennedy Pike
August, 2005

---

[1]. This is one of the terms I use to refer to "God" at work within us. Other terms used throughout with the same meaning are creative force, power to be conscious, Original One, and Power.

[2]. An American Master. Learn more about him online at www.vitvan.org or write to the School of the Natural Order, PO Box 150, Baker, NV 89311.

Words about

Esoteric Astrology

A System of Symbols Representing the Stages of Awakening

In this book I use a metaphor, the House of Self, to describe the energetic structure of the individual. To help explain the energetic openings that occur during the process of awakening, I also use two widely recognized symbol systems, the Chakra System of Yoga and the Seven Rays used in most Wisdom Teachings.

There is another widely recognized system of symbols that has been used for millennia to represent the effect of the cosmic forces on human consciousness, namely, **Esoteric Astrology**. Since many readers may be familiar with the symbolism of astrology, I thought it worthwhile to include a description of the process of awakening according to that system. Since other readers may *not* know astrology and may not have any interest in it, I have placed the astrological symbolism in special inserts at the end of sections or chapters.

Esoteric astrology is not so much a science as it is a complex system of symbols developed by perceivers to teach the essence of the cosmic rays and their effect on and their expression through human beings. It is important to remember that all symbol systems are figurative, not literal. That caveat is as applicable to astrology as to the other symbols I use in this book. If we think of them as real in some objective sense we defeat the purpose set out for this book, which is to think of our life process and ourselves as various states of energy.

Esoteric astrology is not intended to be a scientific description of constellations of stars and the movements of the planets, moon and sun through those constellations. Rather, esoteric astrology is *a symbolic map of the journey each of us makes as we undergo the individualizing process*, the process of awakening to know ourselves as microcosmic representations of the One Self. The constellations, planets, moon and sun are used as *symbols* of the streams of cosmic force that move through our energy fields, of the various stages we move through in the awakening process, and of states of consciousness we will experience and express in the course of our unfolding.

It is not that we will go through these experiences because we are under the influence of the stars and their position at the time of our birth or during any given period of our lives. It is, rather, that *as we move through the individualizing process, we will be able to track our progress and understand the lessons we are learning by reference to this symbolic map.*

The individualizing process represents one phase of the cosmic process. Each of us will move through it. Perceivers in earlier times wanted to give us a way to understand the process, and they developed this symbol system, thinking it would be easy to remember because of its reflection in the nighttime sky. At the time this map was laid out, only seven planets had been identified in

Esoteric Astrology v

our solar system. Consequently, only seven planets were used in the map. Since 1781, three (possibly four, as of 2004) more planets have been discovered. We can think of them as representing the growth in our group consciousness, which is able to register more refined frequencies of energy now.

Esoteric astrology is one of the treasures stored in our subconsciousness, the metaphorical basement of the House of Self. If we learn to appreciate and understand these symbols, we will be able to register intuitively their relevance and application at various stages of our individualizing.

However, we should not say to ourselves, for example, "Jupiter is in Sagittarius (having referred to an astrological chart); therefore, I am experiencing an opening of my Generative Chakra." Rather, we should say, "The strong urge to pursue this particular expression of my creativity with such passion and devotion must be what the ancients referred to as Jupiter in Sagittarius."

In Illustration #12 (page 239), the lunar phase of the individualizing process, as described on page 68 and following, is plotted out on the right side of the page (to the left of the human figure represented there, since the left side of the body is the yin, or lunar, side).

When the ancient seers developed their map of the individualizing process utilizing astrological symbols, they were conscious of outlining an inner journey, not the outward procession of the constellations across the skies. Therefore in esoteric astrology the lunar phase of the process is symbolized as the Journey of the Moon from Sagittarius to Cancer (clockwise). This is the reverse of the Moon's apparent journey through the heavens, which is counterclockwise from Cancer to Sagittarius. Also, in symbolizing this phase of the awakening process by the Moon's journey from Sagittarius to Cancer, Leo was omitted. This is because Leo was assigned to the more advanced phase of the process symbolized by the Sun's journey.

Once the yin/yang forces have reached the Third Eye Chakra in the awakening process, a reorientation occurs in which the entire energy field is polarized to the Crown Chakra. This means that each of the chakras must be reoriented to reflect the Light coming from the Crown Chakra. During this process, the yin/yang forces descend, further clearing the way for the kundalini force. It rises from the Sacral Chakra through the central channel of the spinal cord (called the sushumna in yogic philosophy), passing through each of the chakras till the yin and yang unite in the Crown Chakra. (See the symbols on the left side of Illustration #12, to the right, or conscious side, of the figure represented there.)

The House of Self

THE HOUSE OF SELF

> *Rest assured that if we do not consciously control the forces by which we are motivated, we will be unconsciously controlled by them.*
>
> — *Vitvan*

> *We live in an energy world, and the vehicle through which we live is a dynamic energy field. Therefore, to live in consciousness of self, we need to become skilled at registering and directing the energy that comprises the vehicle of self.*
>
> —Mariamne Paulus

1
The House of Self

We are conditioned to think of the world we live in as a collection of things and objects rather than as fields within fields within fields of energy formed on invisible, archetypal patterns as modern scientists have established. And we are conditioned to think of ourselves as objects among the other objects. So we go through our days imagining that we are separate from the world around us and that the people and things that have an impact on us *cause* our experiences.

We think of ourselves as living in an objective reality, that is, a reality that is physical, material, substantial, and even solid. In fact most of us have grown up thinking and believing that only the tangible is real. If we cannot confirm something's existence through our five physical senses, then we are predisposed to suspect that it doesn't exist at all and is not real. This is what makes it difficult for many people to "believe" in God, life after death, and other doctrines taught by churches. There is no *tangible* proof for what is taught.

A concomitant belief is that because we observe and experience this material world through our five senses, we are quite separate from it and are therefore impartial in our understanding of it. Thus most of us assume that the way we see and understand the world is the way others see and understand it and, in fact, is *the way it is.* Most of us are inclined to think that if anyone understands things differently, they are wrong and we are right. However, some of us think the reverse: that because *we* see and understand things differently from the majority, the *majority* must be right and we are wrong. The underlying premise is the same for both groups: there is only one true way to see and understand the world.

To be told, then, that we are living in an energy world comprised of fields within fields formed on invisible and intangible lines of force doesn't mean much to most of us. We can't see or touch or taste energy; we only know the effects it produces, like heat and light. But we know those effects primarily through physical instruments like electric lamps and stoves that enable us to harness the energy. Therefore, we remain at least once removed from the energy itself, or so it would seem.

When individuals report experiences that we are not able to confirm with our five senses, we are prone, due to our conditioning, to dismiss their reports as subjective, implying that they are not real or valid for the rest of us. Thus we often relegate direct experiences of the energy world to the realm of the elusive, mysterious, and obscure. We tend to dismiss them as peculiar to the individual, having very little value or importance beyond that individual.

Yet our scientists and engineers continue to explore the realm of the intangible and to learn the laws that are at work there. Applying those laws, they are able to do remarkable things, such as to send instruments out into space that transmit data back to earth, describing what they find and sending photographs to confirm the data.

Or they clone the genes of animals and humans. Or they identify which chromosomes in DNA molecules cause particular diseases. Or they photograph stars being born on the periphery of the cosmos. Or they examine the inside of our bodies without cutting them open. In all these instances, scientists are working in the realm of the unseen and, for the most part, we tend to trust their reports and discoveries.

If this kind of mastery of the world around us is possible for scientists, applying laws they have learned to the intangible, why can't we learn to master the seemingly small realms of our own energy fields? There must be laws at work in our fields just as in the rest of this energy world in which we live. By studying those laws we could certainly learn how to work with them to do remarkable things in our own lives.

In the pages that follow, I hope to inculcate a new way of thinking about the world around us and about ourselves. After all, we *are* energy inseparable from the fields of energy in which we are integrated, as any class in chemistry or physics will demonstrate. Therefore, all we do and think and feel takes place in and as energy. If we can learn to *think* the way we actually *function*, rather than thinking that we are solid objects moving about in a material world, then we will be able to grasp the laws at work in us and learn to master the course of our daily lives.

What Are We?

To change the way we now think, we must begin with how we think about ourselves. What are we, really? Most of us think of ourselves as the body and personality in and through which we are living, rather than thinking of ourselves as the power that is *conscious* of the body and personality. By reflecting for a moment on how we actually function, we see that in fact it is as if we are *watching* ourselves. It is as if we can see and hear ourselves as we move through the world, and we are also able to talk to ourselves about ourselves internally.

We can observe and comment on our own bodies and personalities in much the same way as we observe and comment about others and the world around us. Thus it seems that we have a similar relationship to self as we have to others. Since we can observe the body and personality as if from a vantage point within or outside of them, it seems logical that we are functioning *through* the body and personality, observing, registering, directing, and learning from the life experiences we are having.

The Wisdom Tradition has long taught that each of us is ***a point or center of conscious awareness within a dynamic energy field, which in turn is held within larger energy fields.*** As that center of consciousness, we are able to learn how to co-create the reality we live in.

Who Built the House of Self?

To begin to understand the energy fields in and through which we live, let us use a metaphor. Imagine that each human energy field is something like a physical house that is three stories high and has a full basement. We can draw parallels between the image of the three-story house and our seemingly intangible and elusive fields of energy in order to expand our way of thinking about ourselves.

Let us imagine that our birth fathers and mothers carried out the basic construction of our personal houses. With the help of extended families along genetic lines, and using materials provided by the larger community, including materials from other parts of the world, our parents dug a basement and built the foundation for a house. Then, following the architectural plan that had been used to build their own houses, they put up the framework for a three-storied house.

In our metaphor, our fathers and mothers represent the individual energy fields that gave of their own energy substance so that our fields could emerge. The extended families, larger community, and the world represent the larger fields in which we were integrated. Our fields took form according to a universal pattern for human beings held in those larger fields. However, that energy carried the particular qualities and characteristics of the ethnic and cultural groups into which we were born. For example, a house in one part of the world might be made of mud bricks baked in the sun, in another part of the world of the skins of animals, and in still other parts of the world of blocks of ice, logs, boards and plaster, concrete, or glass. In a similar fashion, each energy field emerges from within a particular group field within even larger fields.

In our ordinary way of understanding, we think of physical characteristics as being passed along to us through the genes carried by our physical parents. Those genes have both dominant and recessive characteristics, so that not all children born of the same parents look alike. Yet the characteristics can be traced back, sometimes to a previous generation, and are recognizably typical of the maternal or paternal lineage. Another way to speak of this is to say that each individual field conforms to an archetypal pattern and also carries characteristics of the group fields from which it is formed.

To return to the metaphor of building a house, the parents provide the basic framework for the house by lending their energy substance so that units of energy can gather around the invisible lines of force that form the archetypal human pattern.

What Is the Framework of a Human Energy Field?

In terms of what we can register with our five senses, the framework of the House of Self is the physical body. This is the aspect of our vehicle of self with which we are most familiar, but we think of it almost entirely as an object. In fact, our Western medicine approaches the body as if it had been assembled part by part. A brain, a spinal column and a network of nerves, plus a heart with accompanying veins and arteries, plus a digestive system composed of esophagus, stomach, intestines and rectum, plus a liver, kidneys and a bladder, sexual organs, glands, a bony skeleton with tendons and muscles, plus skin to cover it all — these form a body. Should any of those parts become damaged, they can be removed and either replaced or bypassed. This approach only contributes to our difficulty in grasping with our conscious awareness that what we call the physical body is only our *image* of the basic structure of the human energy field. In reality, the basic structure is energetic.

Let us use the metaphor of the house to help us to think differently about the body.

The basement of the house is buried in the earth and provides the foundation for the building that will stand above ground. Symbolically, this represents our total integration in the human energy field, which is held by the larger fields out of which it emerges: the mineral, plant, and animal fields, as they are commonly called in our Western world.

The vast field that represents the first emergence of form in what we call the physical realm cannot be directly perceived by our physical senses. It consists of the fundamental building blocks of the forms we do perceive with our senses. Scientists have identified and named those building blocks particles, quarks, atoms, molecules, etc.

This large fundamental field lent its energetic substance to the formation of the mineral field, which in turn lent its energetic substance to the formation of the plant field, which in turn lent its energetic substance to the formation of the animal field, which in turn lent its energetic substance to the formation of the human field. And this process is repeated each time a human energy field emerges. From the moment the sperm and egg merge, a chemical process is set in motion that moves, over the course of just weeks, from the molecular to the mineral to the plant to the animal to the human field as the fetus takes form. [Illustration #1]

Thus, by the time the foundation of the house is laid and the framework of the three-story house has been raised, a supportive structure is in place around and within which an elaborate home can be built. In the individual, the physical body is that supportive structure. It consists of an invisible pattern around which are gathered units of energy capable of expressing in form and movement **the four basic functions of human consciousness: sensing, feeling, thinking, and knowing.** In the Wisdom Teachings,[1] **these four functions have**

---

1. See the author's *Awakening to Wisdom*, Scottsdale, AZ: Teleos Imprint, 2002.

Fields Within Fields

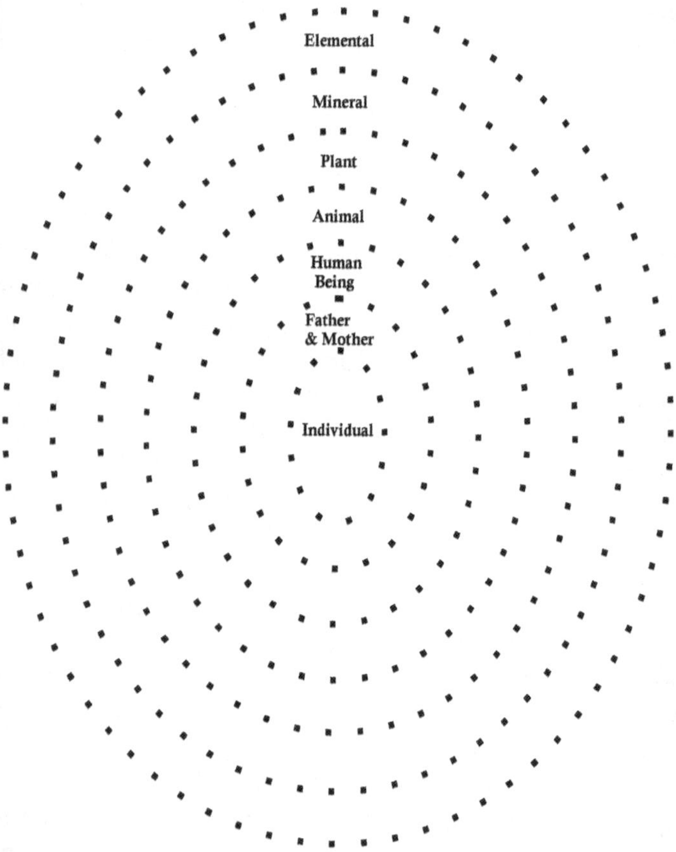

- Elemental
- Mineral
- Plant
- Animal
- Human Being
- Father & Mother
- Individual

Illustration #1

traditionally been correlated with four groupings of what were called the elemental substances, or essences: **earth, water, air, and fire.** As we move forward in our description of the energetic structure of the individual, we will refer to these essential elements as symbols for how we function.

Who Builds the Rest of the House?

The completion of the first and second stories of the house, and even some of the furnishing of those two floors, is a communal affair. The parents are supported by their other children, relatives, schoolteachers, civil authorities, religious officials, friends, and eventually even peers of the growing individual as they help to complete the structure. There are communal codes and laws that apply, governing construction of the house. Matters of preference and taste come into play. In some communities, bright paints might be applied to the exterior of the house; in others, more subdued exteriors are preferred. In some groups, the exterior of the house is not seen as important, so little is done to make it beautiful, but the interior of the building is developed according to group traditions and tastes. As we drive or walk through neighborhoods, we recognize common sizes, styles, and finishes on homes. If a house is dramatically different from the rest of the neighborhood, it not only stands out, but it is often considered out of place, as if it violates a strong preference for uniformity within given communities.

The metaphor helps us to understand the building of the human psyche, or soul, which is symbolized by the first two stories of the house. As we have seen, the foundation and framework of the house are analogous to the physical body. Energetically, the body represents the fundamental pattern of the human energy field. Around that pattern and interpenetrating it, a psyche or soul is formed.

The psyche is comparable to the walls of the house. The walls not only complete the external appearance of the house, but they also give definition to the interior space. Because of the walls we know what belongs to the private life of the individual who lives in the house (the interior space) and what aspects of the house are communal (the exterior of the house).

In a similar fashion, the psyche/soul gives definition to the developing individual. We usually speak of the psyche as the personality. Even though the physical form represents the archetypal pattern of human beings, each body takes on unique characteristics as the personality develops. We can see the effects of the personality reflected in the body, in posture, in the walk, in facial expressions, and in patterns of movement and expression. These effects are something like the paint or stucco on the exterior of a house. They are what the neighbors see and find pleasing or displeasing to their preferences. Meanwhile, many of the personal preferences and opinions of the individual, defining elements of the personality, are held within in the privacy of the inner self.

The process of building a personality, or developing a psyche, begins in the mother's womb, analogous to the basement in our metaphor, with rudimentary sensing, corresponding to what we later call the sense of touch. The development of the psyche progresses rapidly after birth. The differentiation of the sense of touch into sight, hearing, taste and smell marks the expanding **sensing function**, which has traditionally been associated with the element of **earth**, in which the metaphorical basement is buried. The coordination of the sense of touch with the movement of the body also unfolds rapidly during the first two years.

Patterns of response to other people and to life experiences are formed in the early years of the child's life, leading to what we identify as the unique personality of the individual child.

The first story of the metaphorical house represents the **feeling function,** in traditional teachings correlated with the element of **water.** The patterns of the experience and expression of feelings develop rapidly in the first seven years, making it clear that this child is different from all others even though it is obviously a human just like everyone else. The archetypal human pattern determines the structure and function of the physical body. When the personality pattern begins to emerge in the feeling function, it is only secondarily reflected in the body.

As the first story of the house is being structurally completed, the second story is also being built. The second story represents the **thinking function,** associated with the element of **air.** It is the second defining aspect of the psyche. As the thinking function develops during childhood and the teen years, other distinct characteristics of the personality are formed. Interaction between feeling and thinking prods each to develop further. If desires form on the feeling level of the House of Self, the thinking function develops plans for how to fulfill those desires. If the thinking function learns of new possibilities for creative expression, such as new job opportunities or new artistic or scientific disciplines, feelings of desire or longing are aroused that motivate the individual to explore the new and as yet unknown.

Most personalities are greatly influenced during their development by their parents, siblings, teachers, relatives, neighbors, religious officials and peers. Great pressures are brought upon them to conform to the preferences, styles, practices, morals and mores of the groups within which they live. Individuals who do not conform stand out and are often criticized and even ostracized by those around them. One of the strongest motivating forces for most psyches is the urge to please others and win their approval. It is for that reason that we say that the first and second stories of the House of Self are built largely by others.

During the construction of the first two stories of the house, a roof is added to keep the house safe from changing environmental conditions. Under the roof lies an undeveloped attic that will be completed once the person who lives in the house feels the need or the urge to have more space to live in. [Illustration #2]

What Does the Attic Represent?

The development of the third story of the house is provided for in the archetypal pattern or design. However, neither the parents nor the larger community can build this part of the house. The resident is the only one who can develop the third story.

The third story represents the **knowing function,** linked with the element of **fire.** If the framework symbolizes what we call the physical body, and the first and second stories of the house correspond to the personality (or psyche, or soul), then the third story represents the spirit (or higher self). Many persons never develop this upper story. The potential is there, but they don't get around to it in the course of their living.

When we have developed the first and second stories of the House of Self fully enough to feel we have ex-

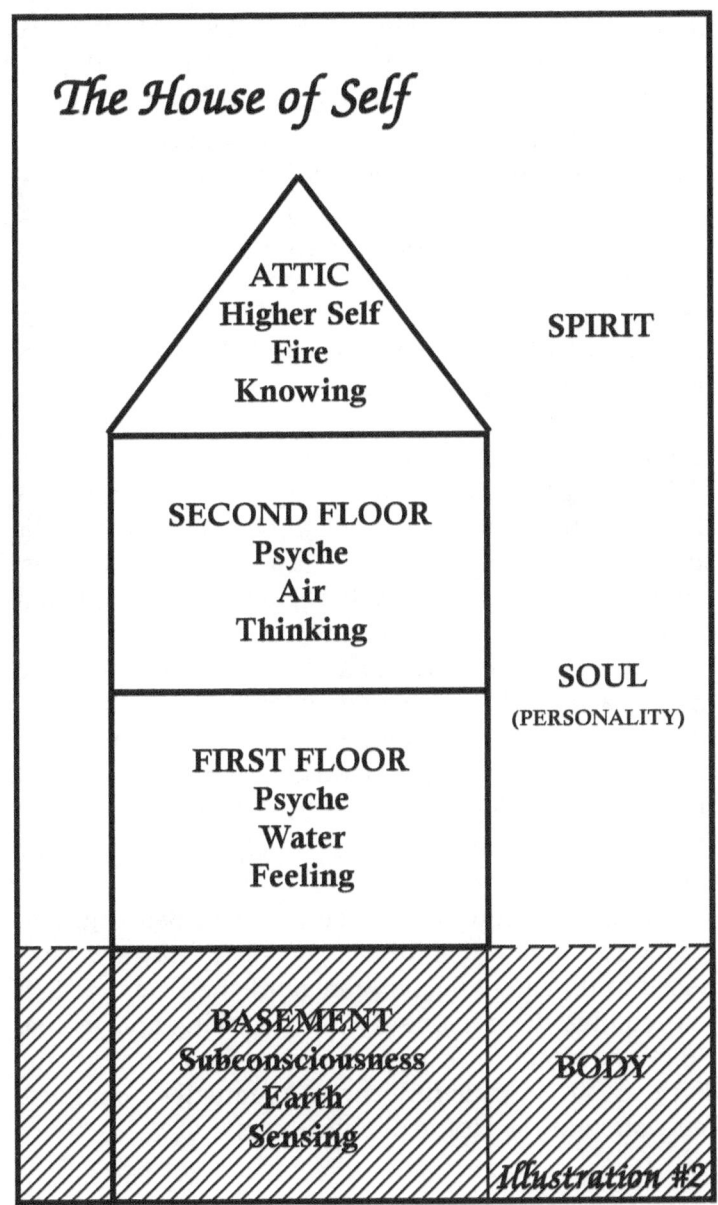
Illustration #2

plored most of the possibilities available to us, then we long for something more. When we *feel* that something is missing in our lives, then with our *thinking* function we explore what that could be. As we talk to other people, read books, attend lectures, and listen within, we discover there is a whole new realm of possibility available to us. **We can develop spiritually, awakening our knowing function.** From the second story of the house we build a stairwell into the attic. We are able to climb that stairwell with a higher aspect of the thinking function. It takes us into the realm of knowing.

Some people develop the attic without altering the exterior of the house. In that case, neighbors have no way of knowing that there is anything different about this house from the others on the block. The individual's spiritual life remains private and is not revealed to others, and the roof keeps her safe during all the inner environmental changes that are sure to occur.

Others put windows in and raise the roof to make more space for the knowing function. These individuals are recognized as different. Some people are drawn to these individuals and ask questions about what makes them different from the rest of the community in which they live. Others avoid them precisely *because* they are different.

Once the third story of the House of Self begins to be developed, new qualities and characteristics are introduced to the internal environment of the House of Self that change the personality. The thinking and feeling functions begin to respond more to the energy of the spirit than to outside influences. Eventually a complete renovation of the House of Self occurs.

The House of Self

How Do Our Energy Fields Differ from the House Metaphor?

There is one major difference between a physical house, such as we have been using as our metaphor, and the House of Self, which is made of energy. The physical house is three-dimensional and the energy field is at least four-dimensional. This means that our image of the house is layered, each level stacked on top of the one beneath it. The third story is seen to be the highest up. In our objective reality, we often consider the highest as the best or the most developed.

The energy field, however, is not layered. It is, rather, four primary fields of energy nested together, interpenetrating one another. In the early stages of development the frequencies represented by the physical body surround and protect the developing psyche. When the psyche (personality) is more fully formed and has more definition, the physical frequencies become more transparent so that the psyche can shine through.

When the frequencies of spirit begin to resonate in the consciousness of the individual, they are often experienced as buried deep within, at the heart of self. There they remain quite invisible and inaccessible to others until they expand and grow stronger. [Illustration #3]

In the Wisdom Teachings, these nested fields have often been called "bodies," using the analogy of the physical body to make reference to the more intangible vehicles of expression. In this electronic era, it is easier to grasp the concept of energy fields, even when our thinking function is still wedded to images of the physical body as "solid."

At a certain stage in the development of the individual, a reversal occurs. It is as if the energy field is turned inside out. The spirit comes out to the periphery,

18 THE HOUSE OF SELF

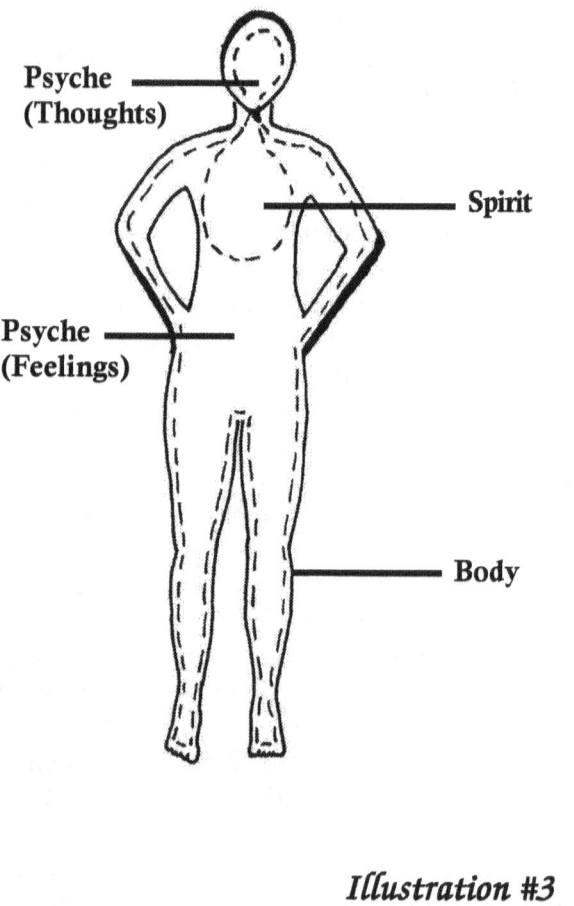

Illustration #3

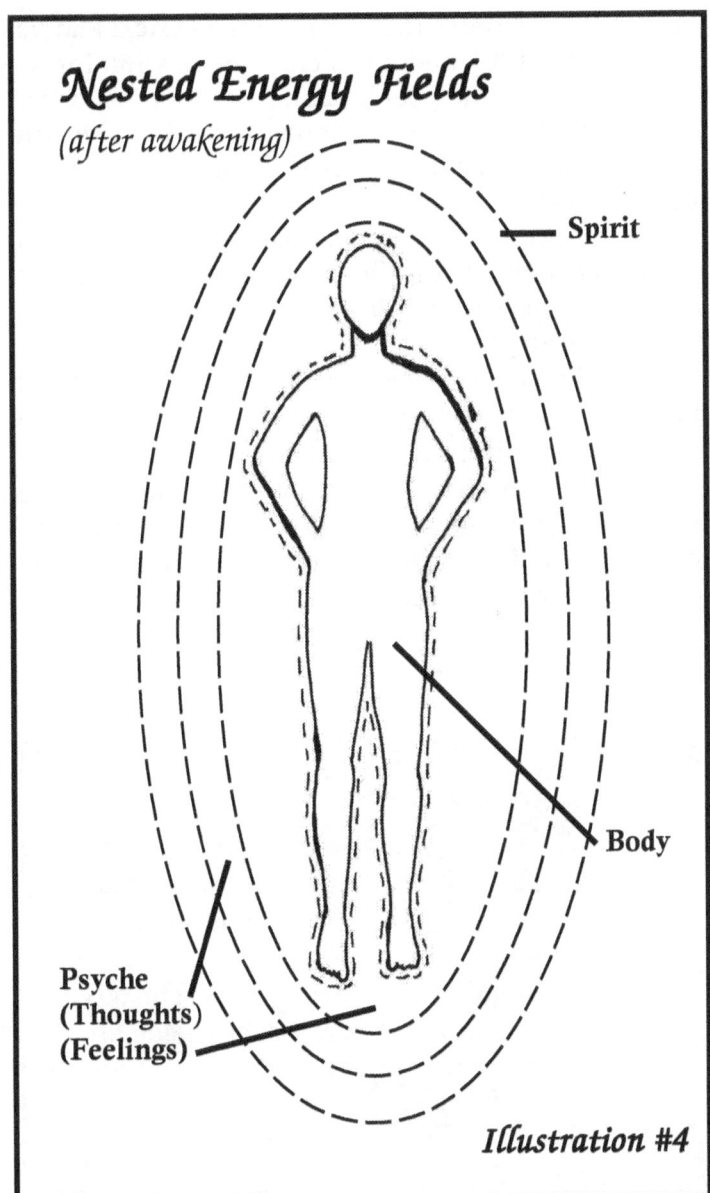

Illustration #4

the psyche penetrates the walls of the physical and becomes both a filter and a vehicle of expression for the spirit, and the archetypal human pattern on which the physical body was built is drawn inward to the core where it acts as an axis on which all four fields turn. [Illustration #4]

When we speak of the human energy field, then, we are speaking of four fields nested together as one. These are fields within fields, coordinated and interpenetrating one another.

It is difficult to represent this four-dimensional field on paper, but as we explore each of the four energetic functions more deeply, I hope that you will begin to *feel* the difference, learn to *think* about it as more than a vehicle moving through space, and come to *know* what it is to register and direct energy consciously as you co-create your everyday experiences.

Ways to Practice:
To change your way of thinking about yourself and to become more conscious of yourself as energy, engage in these simple exercises.

1. Sit quietly and focus on your breathing. Each time you inhale, *feel* the air entering your body. Begin to imagine that your entire body is becoming air. As you let go of the sensation that the body is solid, let the sensation of the body as air replace it. Then begin to affirm: *this body is energy, moving, flowing, and changing like air.*

2. As you sit quietly, focused on your breathing, remember that energy can produce heat. Rub your hands together. Then separate them slightly, continuing to rotate them next to each other in small circles. Keep breathing consciously.

    a. See if you can feel the heat your own energy field produces. Then experiment to see how far you can pull your hands apart before you stop feeling the heat.

    b. Rub your hands together again, and this time when you separate them, imagine you have a ball of energy between them. Begin to work with this ball, breathing energy into it as your hands move closer together and farther apart until you can actually sense the substance of the energy.

    c. Finally, take your hands up to your head and face. Without actually touching yourself, sense the energy around your head and face. How far can you move your hands away from the head before you lose touch with the energy?

3. As you sit quietly, aware of your breathing, bring the sounds in your environment into focus. Let them move through you instead of thinking about them. Feel them touch your energy field and then pass through it. Don't bother to label the sound. Experience it as a vibration or frequency wave passing through your field of awareness. How does it affect your field as it passes through? Is it sharp or smooth, disruptive or harmonious, gentle or rough? What other descriptive words would you use to describe each sound that passes through?

4. While sitting quietly and attending to your breathing, taste a few foods. Don't think of the names of the foods. Instead see if you can describe the effect of the food on your energy field as you did with sounds in number 3 above. Imagine that the taste of the food is a vibration moving through your field. How would you describe the vibration?

5. Do this same exercise with different scents in your environment and with different colors as you look at them. Observe the scents and colors as vibrations moving through your field and find descriptive words for the effect they have on your field.

6. Throughout each day, whenever you touch anything, say to yourself, "This is a configuration of units of energy." Even if you cannot experience it as energy, as vibrations moving through your field, *think of it* that way.

Notes:

2
Force and Form

To develop a new way of thinking and speaking about the physical body, we begin with the recognition that it is not a thing. It is, rather, a dynamic field of units of energy that have been attracted to a vibrating pattern, and thus have taken on a recognizable form. With our objective minds, we view the body's form as solid, but in the energy world it is completely permeable. Just as the earth can, to the senses, seem solid until we pour water on it, so the energies of the body were relatively hard (condensed, or concentrated) until the psyche began to permeate them, causing them to expand and become more porous. Some say that on Atlantis, humans had bodies that seemed as hard as iron. That implies that their psyches were relatively undeveloped and were still held within the physical field, protected from and seemingly invisible to the outside world.

In our age, most human bodies are quite soft to the touch, even when the muscles are highly developed. This is a sign that the psyches are sufficiently developed to permeate the physical envelope, if not to extend beyond it. Or perhaps it would be more accurate to say that we have learned to perceive *more* than objective reality (what can be registered by the five senses) and thus bodies seem softer to the touch. This reflects the growing capacity of our consciousness to register more subtle energies. The quality of "softness" is actually a reflection of our state of consciousness, which no longer perceives the body to be solid.

So let us begin by thinking of the body as an energetic pattern rather than as a physical body. The pattern would be entirely invisible to us if molecules of energy had not gathered around it. We cannot, for example, see the pattern a sound makes. But if we place grains of sand on a drumhead and then strike the drum, the granules of sand will form a pattern, the pattern of the vibration the sound is making. In a similar fashion, energy gathers around the invisible pattern of a human being and we recognize the person as one of our species. [Illustration #5]

Running through this energetic pattern are streams of force that we identify objectively as circulation of blood, inhalation and exhalation of air, ingestion and digestion of food, circulation of lymphatic fluids, and transmission of sensory data on nerve pathways. If you can let go of the labels and dissolve the edges on these conceptual images, you can imagine energy in constant movement that is held within the form of the pattern, like water within the banks of a river. In the same way as the water of a river sometimes seems caught in eddies or whirlpools, and yet keeps moving, so the energy of the physical frequency band of the human field moves along currents that we call veins and arteries, or nerve pathways, or breathing passages, and yet it is constantly intermingling and changing pathways. For example, oxygen is carried first on the breath, then by the blood, and finally is distributed

The Body as an Energy Pattern

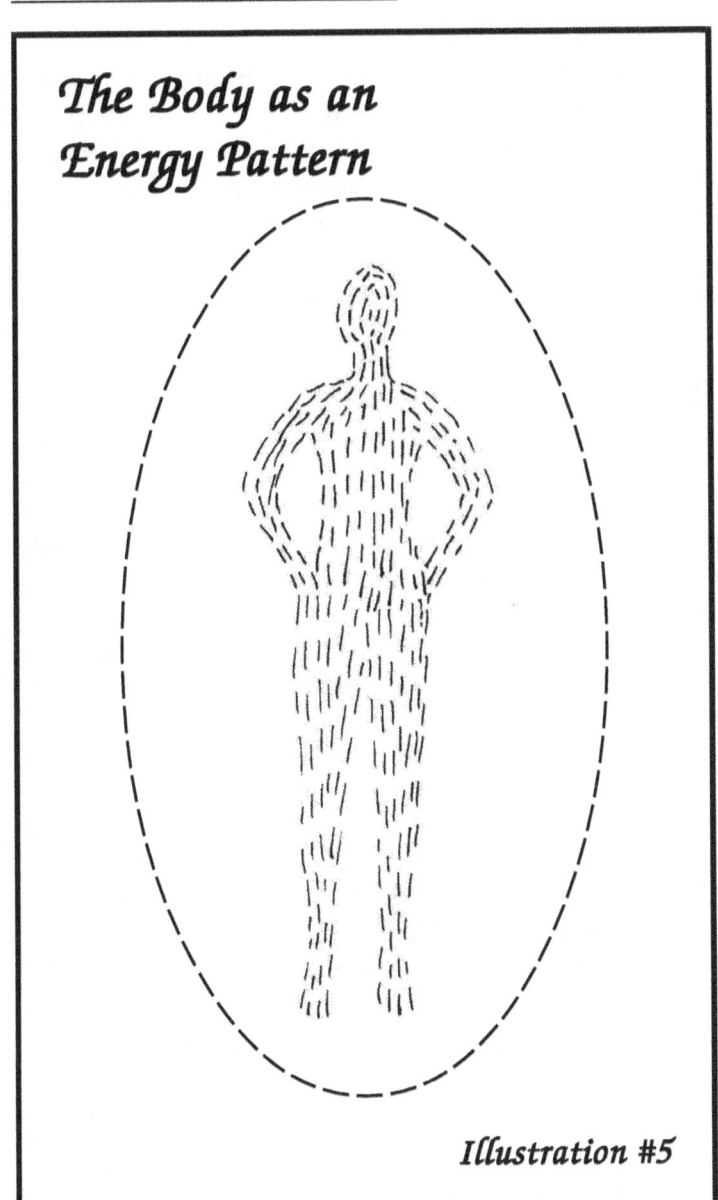

Illustration #5

throughout the entire field.

The Hermetic principle of vibration,[1] namely, that everything is always in motion, is in evidence in the human energy field. In the physical frequencies, changes are constant and never-ending because everything is in motion. All day, every day, the physical body is being energetically renewed and is changing to give expression to the psyche and the spirit.

How Can We Talk About The Energy Moving Through Our Field?

We are learning to think the way we function. We function as energy fields, with streams of force moving in patterns that are recognizable. How can we identify those energies without resorting to objective images or descriptions?

First of all, we need to think in terms of **force and form.** Units of energy gather along the lines of invisible patterns, and those patterns are what we call **forms.** To have an image of an invisible pattern, think of the patterns revealed when ice crystals form on windows in cold weather. The molecules of water in the moist air gather on invisible patterns to form crystals. Once the crystals have taken form, we can "see" the pattern that was invisible before then. Or, place iron filings on a piece of glass. Then run a magnet beneath the

---

1. Hermes Trismegistus formulated seven principles to describe the energetic functions of consciousness in our universe. These Hermetic principles have been fundamental to Wisdom Teachings for millennia. The principles are Mentalism, Correspondences, Vibration, Polarity, Rhythm, Cause and Effect, and Gender. See the author's *Awakening to Wisdom*, page 16.

glass. The iron filings will take the form of the pattern of the magnetic energy.

In many science museums and earth stores you can see examples of particles of energy gathering on invisible patterns. This phenomenon is one of the awe-inspiring mysteries of the natural world. ***Energy gives form to otherwise invisible patterns.***

Force is the invisible power that carries the pattern and activates the energy so that it comes into a **form**.

To be conscious of the energy world we need to learn to identify the **force** that brings **form** into being. Within our own energy fields, one way we experience force is as an *urge* that causes us to take some action through the physical body. It is a *motivating force*. For example, adrenaline reflects a **force** that motivates us to take swift action, often in the **form** of either fight (standing up for oneself, or defending oneself) or flight (running away). We often think that a feeling of fear motivates us to fight or flee. But adrenaline functions beneath the surface of our self-consciousness, and the *feelings* that surface in our awareness actually *follow* the impulse to sudden movement activated by adrenaline.

Motivating forces that move through subconsciousness and get expressed in and through the physical body are called instincts. They draw on the wisdom gathered from millennia of experience in the plant, animal, and human energy fields. They move our bodies into action whether we have conscious awareness of what is happening or not. We experience this kind of instinct when we recoil from a sharp or hot object. Before we can register in our conscious awareness a threat to the well being of our bodies, the body itself is moved by instinct to pull back from harm.

Another instinct is the urge to procreate. Often against the best judgment of the psyche, sexual energies are aroused and the urge to procreate takes the **form** of sexual intercourse. This is not about attraction on the level of personality or spirit. It is about a powerful, life-giving **force** that seeks to make sure the human species survives.

Another **force** moving through us on the physical level is hunger. It takes the **form** of ingesting and digesting food. The **force** of thirst takes the **form** of drinking fluids, the **force** of breathlessness, the **form** of inhaling.

These various instinctual urges are activated within the human energy field at birth. The infant doesn't need to be taught to breathe, to suckle at the mother's breast, or to cry when it experiences discomfort. Forces move from within subconsciousness to motivate these expressions of the will to live.

Another fundamental **force** is experienced as the urge to move. It takes **form** as physical activity and expression. This is the principle of vibration brought into more evolved expression. Streams of force within the physical body work together in coordinated movement.

The forces we recognize as instincts continue to work within us as long as we are conscious of the physical band of energy frequencies. We need to learn to identify them and to distinguish them from forces moving in the psyche and in the spirit if we want to make conscious choices about our self-expression.

How Is Power, or Force, Brought Into and Dispersed Through Our Human Fields?

In order for electrical power to be brought into a

house, power lines must be hooked up to generators and then brought to the house where fuses and breakers help to regulate the amount of power made available in the house. Electrical wires are threaded through the walls of the house and connected to electrical outlets and light switches. To use the electricity, either an appliance must be plugged into an outlet or the light switch must be turned on.

Again, the metaphor of the house being wired for electricity helps us to imagine how power is brought to the human energy field. The generator of power is the Original One that rays out the force that eventuates in more forms than can ever be identified or counted. There are **seven principal lines of force**, and they are analogous to high voltage electrical power lines except that they are not physical wires. They are energetic rays like those that stream out from the sun. **The seven rays,** which are invisible to us, have been named Will, Activity, Love-Wisdom, Science, Harmony, Devotion, and Ceremony. The labels suggest the qualities and characteristics associated with each ray, as we will describe below. [See Illustration #6.]

The power of these rays is enormous. They motivate everything in our cosmos. They are the **force** moving in every **form,** including the human field with its four-fold functions.

For the human energy field to be empowered by the seven rays, converters were needed that could lower the voltage to human levels. Thus each human energy field has **seven chakras**[2] to perform that function. A

---

2. Chakra is a Sanskrit word that means "wheel." The science and philosophy of yoga have brought the term to the West and the word *chakra* has now been adopted into English and appears in our dictionaries.

32 THE HOUSE OF SELF

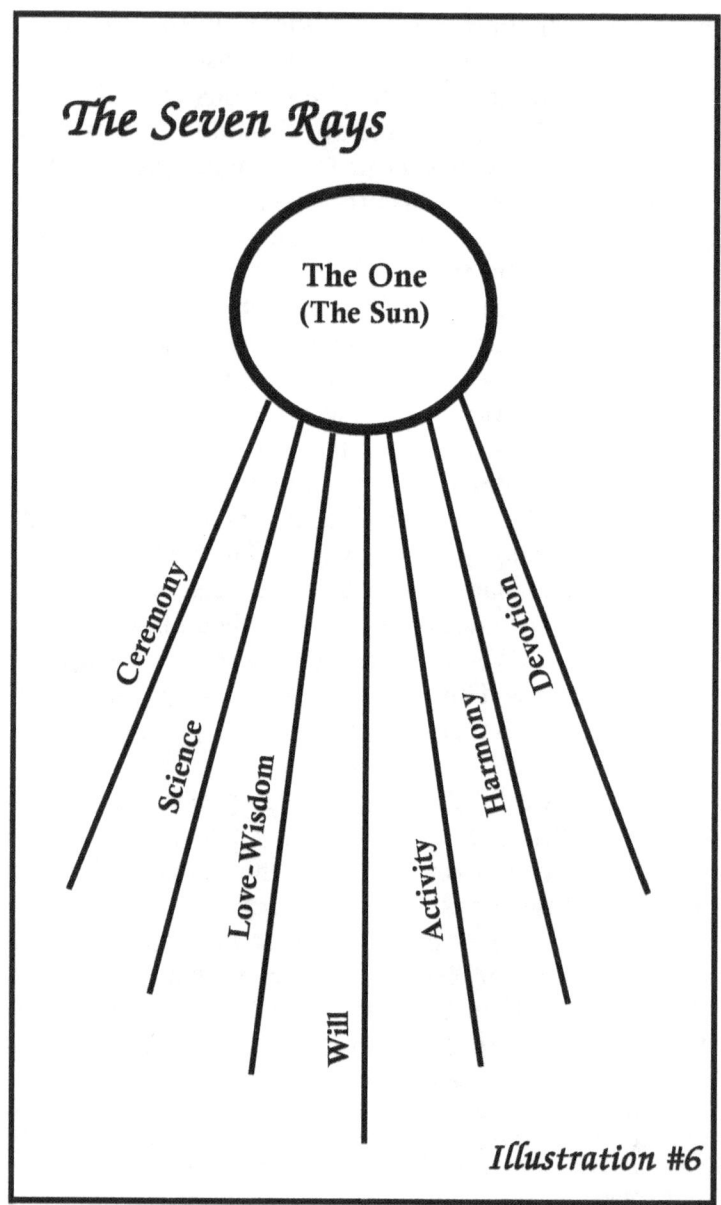

Illustration #6

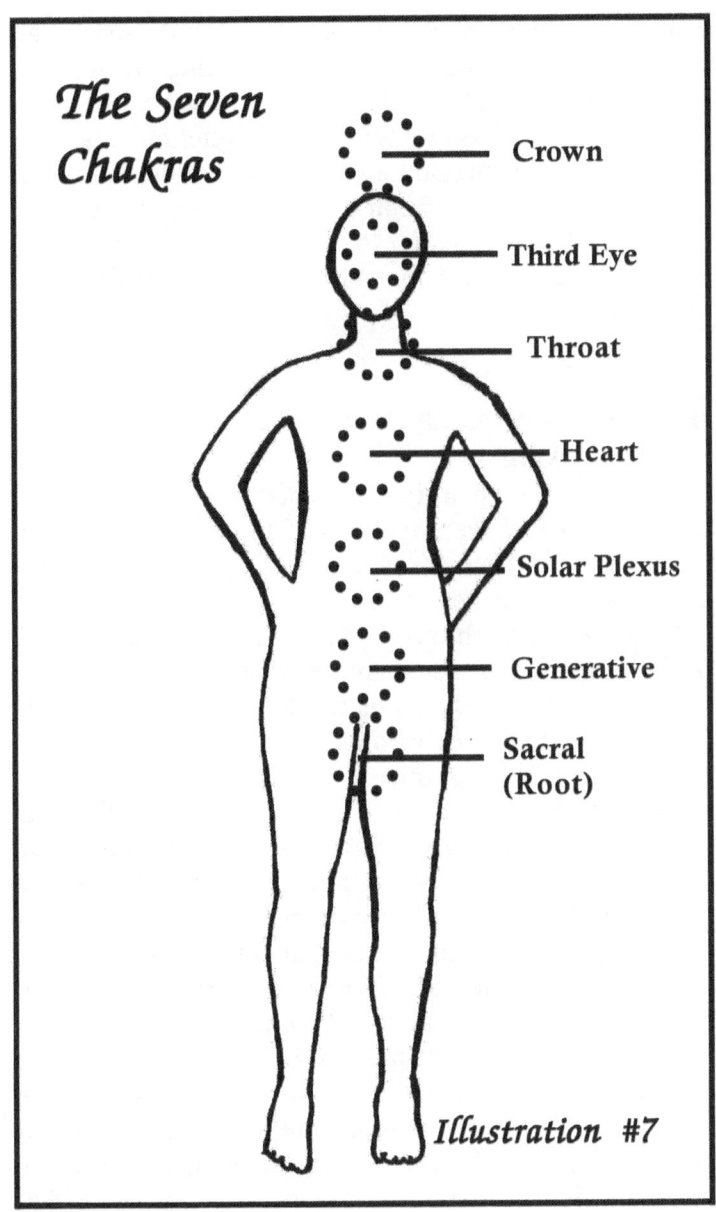

Illustration #7

chakra is a vortex of energy. As it spins, it draws energy in from the corresponding ray and "spins" it out into the individual energy field where it mixes and blends with the other chakra energies at frequencies that are registered and expressed according to the development of the individual. In English these chakras are usually called the Crown, Sacral (or Root), Heart, Third Eye, Solar Plexus, Generative, and Throat Chakras. [Illustration #7]

How Does Our Consciousness of Force and Form Awaken?

Generally speaking, we become conscious of form long before we are aware of force. As our image of the nested fields (see page 18) suggests, we are aware first of the wave band of frequencies that we are able to register with our physical senses. Later we will talk about these senses energetically, but for now to think of the senses helps us to identify the parameters of the force channeled through the Generative Chakra.

Generally speaking, if we can see, hear, touch, smell or taste something, it has taken **form** within the band of frequencies that correspond to the Generative Chakra. Our physical bodies fall within this category. In the early phases of our development, we learn to identify and give name to forms. But seldom, if ever, are we invited to notice what force brought the form into being or what motivates it to do whatever it does.

We might ask, "Where do rocks come from?" or "What makes a rose bush grow roses rather than apples?" or "Why are frogs different from cats?" In our culture right now there are two competing answers, neither of which explains very much. One answer is that

God created it all. The other answer is that these are the result of evolution. Neither answer gives us an understanding of the how or the why.

The first two rays, called **Will and Activity**, set in motion the whole creating process in which the invisible patterns held as potential in the energies of the **Will Ray,** channeled through the **Crown Chakra,** take on energy substance in the frequencies of the Activity Ray. The forms brought into being on the **Activity Ray,** channeled through the **Sacral Chakra** of human energy fields, cannot be registered by the physical senses. They are not yet tangible. It is only when their vibration is raised into the frequency band of the **Generative Chakra** that our ordinary human consciousness can grasp them.

The process could be likened to the birth of a child. When the sperm and egg unite, a creating process is set in motion in the womb. There are indications that a child is being formed, but without instruments to extend the senses, such as ultrasound, we cannot see what is happening in the womb. Only as the fetus grows and the form becomes more substantial can we begin to feel the infant kicking and moving, and hear the heartbeat. When the fetus leaves the womb and is given birth we are finally able to fully experience it with our five senses.

The womb is analogous to the **Sacral Chakra**. Activity is going on in that chakra that begins to clothe invisible patterns with energy substance. However, until the form manifests as physical, we do not register it in our objective consciousness. Consequently, it is our experience that the **Generative Chakra** is the form-giving chakra, even though the process of coming into form is actually set in motion by the Will and Activity

For an introduction to these inserts on Esoteric Astrology, see pages iii - vi.

Saturn in Capricorn

The astrological symbols associated with the forces released in the earth energies of the Sacral Chakra are **Saturn in Capricorn**. [See Illustration #12, page 239.]

In Greek mythology **Saturn** was the name of the Supreme God, the power behind all forms and activities in the Universe. He is therefore an appropriate symbol for the force known as the **Activity Ray.** It is the nature of this expression of power to bring energy into form and to sustain the process of producing forms until consciousness becomes Self-aware.

Capricorn, the 10th house in the Zodiac, represents a focus on preserving form and providing security. Capricorn symbolizes earth energy. The key words for Capricorn are "**I Use**," calling our attention to our task, which is to learn to use earth energies consciously in our awakening process. Therefore, under the constraints of Saturn we learn how to live in bodies (forms), and how to work with other forms in the frequencies represented by earth energies. For a time during our unfolding we are totally preoccupied with the material aspects of life.

Rays through the Crown and Sacral Chakras. Not until late in our awakening process are we able to register the motivating urges of the Will and Activity Rays.[3]

By the time we become conscious of form, then, we are registering energies that correspond to the Generative Chakra, energies that can be registered with our physical senses. And for the most part, we are not aware of the motivating force that brought the form into being.

How Does Form Serve Our Awakening Consciousness?

Forms make it possible for the Original Power to become aware of Itself. They act as a kind of mirror in which Power, which is invisible, becomes visible. The images in this physical mirror that we call the universe reflect many of the diverse qualities or characteristics inherent in the Original One.

In the cosmic process, energetic forms are fundamental to the experience and expression of consciousness. Consciousness can be defined as the movement of energy in form, that is, in specific patterns. Each form gives expression to a bundle of characteristics of the Originating Power.

In the individualizing process of the human being, forms take on additional significance because they make it possible for each person to become aware of self. That is, consciousness in the human form becomes conscious of being conscious. According to the Wisdom Teachings, the human being represents the beginning of the fulfillment of the deep longing that set

---

3. See Chapters Eleven and Twelve below.

the creating process in motion. That longing was for Self-knowledge.

There is, in this understanding, only one Self. To know Itself, the Original One looks into billions of small mirrors – the forms of the physical universe – and in each mirror it becomes conscious of certain characteristics of Self. Humans represent the beginning of this consciousness of Self, for the One Self looks through the eyes of each individual self.

Human self-consciousness begins with an awareness of the physical body. In the early stages of development, human self-consciousness is not able to perceive the energy itself. Instead we register an overall impression of the energy as it traverses the pathways that conform to the archetypal human pattern. What we see appears in our consciousness to be a solid body.

To grasp how this process works, think of an electric fan. Before the electricity is turned on, the fan is perceived to have several blades. When the power is turned on and the fan begins to spin, the blades appear to melt into a solid, spinning disc. As the velocity increases, the blades seem to disappear and we are able to see right through them. This is because our neural receptors cannot transmit the information rapidly enough to enable us to see the individual blades as they are spinning.

Molecules of energy are spinning even more rapidly than the blades of an electric fan. To our senses, the pathways they travel in the lower frequencies of the physical realm blur into what appear to be solid objects, like the apparently solid spinning fan disc. In the higher frequencies of the psychic and spiritual realms, the molecules travel so fast that we cannot register them at all with our five senses. We, in effect, see right through them just as we can see through the spinning blades of a fan. It is as if the psyche and the spirit are invisible. Some would say nonexistent.

Yet we can register the effect of the presence of the psyche and spirit. Just as a fan moves air and would cut off your finger if you stuck it into the spinning blades that seem invisible, so the effects of soul and spirit can be experienced even though we can't see them. Personalities seem to change the air in a room. We feel different in their presence than before they came in. And the presence of an energetic spirit can enliven, uplift and inspire us like nothing else.

As we experience physical energies through our five senses, then, we register them in our objective consciousness, but only as images, not in their energetic form. It is these images, which are held in our psyches, that enable us to think about what we have perceived, and thus to become conscious that we are conscious.

Forms are essential to the development of our consciousness of self. They serve all four functions of consciousness, sensing, feeling, thinking, and knowing, as we shall discover. We could not develop spiritually without physical energies in which to catch a reflection of what we are coming to know.

In our consciousness of physical energies, the earth element predominates. It helps to anchor us in the experience of form, because it has a tendency to move down in frequency. We often speak of the element of earth as a grounding force, and when people feel ungrounded or lack stability, they can shift their attention to the Generative and Sacral Chakras and consciously direct their energies downward. This will help them to find grounding.

However, all four elements, earth, water, air, and

fire, are essential to form. The higher frequencies interpenetrate the lower frequencies in the same way that water and air suffuse soil, in which the element of earth predominates. Moreover, fire is at the heart of every molecule of energy and therefore is fundamental to all energetic expression.

Our consciousness expands to incorporate higher frequencies that can no longer be registered with our physical senses, but it continues to function in and as physical form until such a time as we can sustain consciousness of self without a "mirror" to look in.

The forms we perceive – the images of those forms held in our psyches – are actually reflections of our own state of consciousness. We live in objective consciousness, perceiving the energy world through the medium of images held in our psyches.

Jupiter in Sagittarius

Again referring to Greek Mythology, Saturn was eventually overthrown by **Jupiter** who was a symbol for the psyche as it began to awaken. Therefore, Jupiter became a symbol for the first force that works with some degree of self-awareness in the human field, namely the force released in the Generative Chakra.

The key words for the sign of **Sagittarius** are "**I pursue**." This represents the early stages of harnessing the subconscious urges of self-preservation with the awareness "I am this body." The activities motivated by the sacral energies are now expressed as personal effort offered in service to the cause of protecting the tribe and one's own offspring in the energies of the Generative Chakra.

The Devotional Ray, released through the Generative Chakra, arouses a *passion for the essential* that the Activity Ray in the Sacral Chakra does not inspire. Persons motivated by the Generative Chakra are willing to do whatever is necessary and to pursue any quest that will fulfill the urge to be of service. They see a goal. They pursue it. They reach it. And then they see another goal that they pursue.

When individuals begin to awaken (Jupiter in Sagittarius), the creative urge of the Generative Chakra expands beyond the urge to procreate. Jupiter in Sagittarius symbolizes the release of abundant, unrestricted energy that can be utilized in any pursuit, whether in the arts, politics, business, education, religion, social reform, science, technology, sports, or whatever.

When Jupiter is in Sagittarius, symbolically, the individual awakens to this creative force and begins to make conscious choices about its expression. We are no longer at the effect of instinctual urges that would send us out to pursue a mate with whom to procre-

> ate. Instead, we recognize the creative force as an urge to bring something new into manifestation, and we pursue avenues of expression for our talents, gifts, and personal interests.

When Do We Become Aware of Force?

Perhaps the earliest awareness most of us have of a force moving in us is experienced in our childhood as the urge to be helpful. Usually we feel this urge first at home, wanting to help our parents in chores around the house. Certainly most of us experience it once we start going to school as an urge to help teachers or fellow classmates. This is our beginning awareness of the **Devotional Ray,** channeled through the **Generative Chakra.** [Illustration #8]

The Generative Chakra energies encompass the spectrum of physical activity, from exercising the body, to gesturing as part of communication, to dance and martial arts, to making things, such as building houses, to birthing babies. Any form of *doing* shares the energies of the Generative Chakra.

The urge to do something ("what can I do to help?") is an awareness of a motivating force, but we may not know more about that force until long into our awakening to the energy world.

The Devotional Ray releases a powerful urge in us, through the Generative Chakra, to be of service. The energies of the individual are devoted to the preservation of the family or tribal unit. Providing food and

Force and Form 43

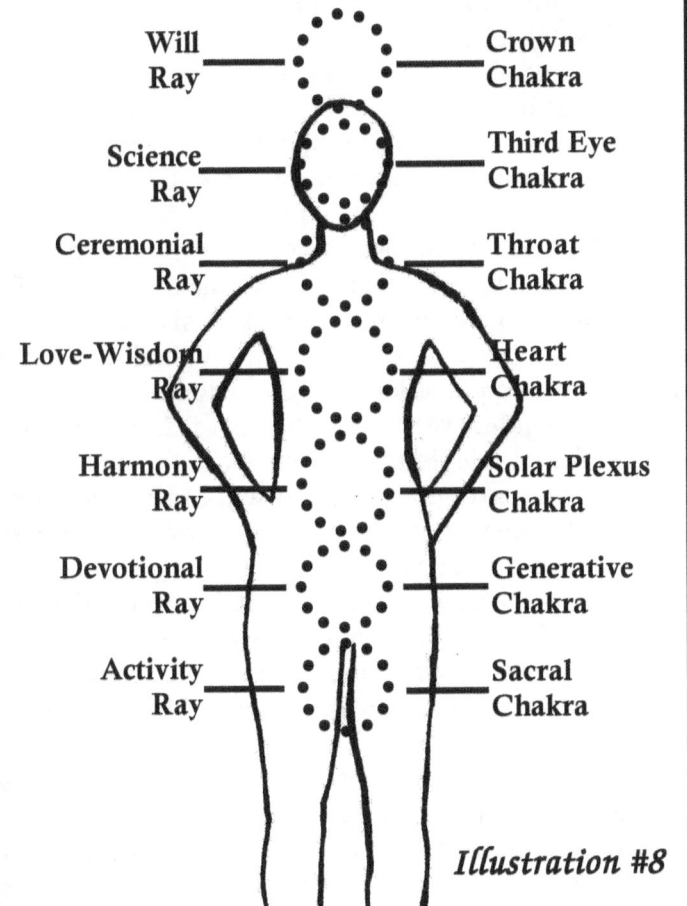

Illustration #8

shelter becomes a way to serve the family and tribe to which one belongs. Devotion manifests as loyalty and often as self-sacrifice, giving up one's life to save the life of the larger group. Devotion is the first force that works with some degree of self-awareness in the human field, even though not necessarily by that name.

Children begin to act out in their play the roles of adults because of their subconscious urge to be of service. Teenagers often undertake service projects as expressions of this urge. The motivating force is so strong that by the teen years it is accompanied by an idealism of what is possible that not only results in setting lofty aspirations for their own lives but also results in harsh criticism of adults whom they feel have "sold out." The Devotional Ray awakens a hunger to make a contribution to the world that will make life better for all people. It leads to intense and persistent devotion to a cause, a purpose, or a given individual that sometimes borders on fanaticism or obsession.

By the adult years, the objects of devotion often change for people, but those in whom the energies of this Ray are particularly strong will blossom as completely devoted to their families, friends, careers, causes, or individuals they admire or the god they worship. They live lives of service that are productive and focused. They are enthusiastic beyond measure about the object of their devotion. They are unwavering in their loyalty and are often characterized by a sacrificial love.

The energies of the Devotional Ray arouse a passion that the Activity Ray does not inspire. Those motivated through the Generative Chakra are willing to do whatever is necessary to fulfill the urge to be of service.

What Is the Symbolic Meaning of the Basement?

In the metaphor of the House of Self, presented in Chapter One, we spoke of the foundation of the house as a basement dug into the earth. The basement represents subconsciousness, which might also be called universal subconsciousness or the collective unconscious. The basement symbolizes all the functions of consciousness that developed prior to our human self-consciousness. Nearly all of the functions of the physical body, for example, are outside our conscious awareness. They are essential to the life of the body. While we are developing our self-consciousness, subconsciousness sustains the vehicle in, through, and as which we are becoming self-conscious. In fact, only the breath is easy for us to control consciously, and using the symbolism of the four elements [Illustration #2] we can see that until we develop our thinking function, which is symbolized by air, we cannot be self-aware or function with self-consciousness. Therefore it makes sense that we should begin with breathing to connect our self-consciousness to the earth energies, as was suggested in the exercises beginning on page 20 .

The body is an expression of all the knowledge accumulated in the evolutionary process before self-consciousness emerged. The body represents sophisticated expressions of consciousness, but we have no conscious access to most of them. Therefore, the symbol of the basement serves to remind us that we have a storehouse of knowledge available to us that is as vast as the evolutionary process itself. As we develop our higher faculties, we will learn how to descend into the basement, so to speak, and register consciously the wisdom of the ages. That is the fruit of awakening to the sacral energies.

Even when we have not yet gained conscious access to the basement, we are being served by the wisdom stored within it. Our bodies are kept alive by that wisdom. When their energy flows are disturbed in some way, causing distortions in the **form,** the **force** reasserts the archetypal pattern in what we call the healing process. But even beyond instinct, we are served by wisdom from subconsciousness through the many forms of insight and intuition. **Everything comes to us through subconsciousness, whether in the form of sensory data, feelings, thoughts, or knowing.** As we grow in consciousness we can learn to draw on that wealth intentionally.

The basement is a metaphor for the secure foundation that the four elements, earth, water, air and fire, provide for the House of Self. On that foundation is built the energetic structure of the individual.

Ways to Practice:

1. Throughout each day, whatever you are doing, **breathe consciously** into the activity and *feel force moving into form.*

2. Sit quietly. As you breathe, **imagine energies being drawn up through your feet** and into the Sacral Chakra surrounding the base of the spinal column and into the Generative Chakra in the area of the groin and the reproductive organs. Be aware as **force** begins to gather there and notice what urges are awakened in you to take action, to **bring something into form.**

3. Observe yourself throughout the day. Identify instinctual urges (force) that arise in you. Think of them as the Activity Ray moving through your subconscious mind, or the Devotional Ray motivating your subconscious mind to bring something into **form**.

4. Observe yourself throughout the day. Identify creative urges (force) that require your conscious direction to bring them into **form.** Think of them as the Activity Ray motivating you, or as the Devotional Ray urging you to conscious expression, according to the nature of the creativity.

Notes:

3
The Creative Force

In our attempt to learn to **think** the way we **function**, namely, to use the language of energy to describe our energetic processes, we are using descriptions developed in the Wisdom Traditions. It is important not to think of these literally, in some objective sense, or we defeat our purpose, which is to think of our life process and ourselves as various states of energy.

When we speak of the **seven energy chakras**, it is important that we not visualize these chakras as occupying a particular space in our energy fields. We associate them with certain parts of the body because of the *function* of the respective organs in the body, not due to a spatial location.

The Generative Chakra, for instance, is characterized by energies vibrating at frequencies that we can register through our physical senses. Since our sexual organs perform the *function* of bringing new physical forms into being, we associate the energies of the Generative Chakra with those organs. However, the Generative Chakra is actually a vortex within our energy field and it disperses the forces of the Devotional Ray throughout that whole field, and the fields within the field.

We must not allow our minds, which love to form

three-dimensional pictures in our psyches, to see the chakras as fixed in space, as located in the physical body, or as in some way dependent on or secondary to the physical body. To the contrary, the generative energies help to sustain the body and to awaken in the psyche the urge to create *through* the body.

Perhaps the safest image to hold in our psyches is of a sphere of energy in which seven vortices are spinning, helping to circulate streams of force throughout the entire field. Of the five vortices that pertain specifically to the functioning of the body and psyche, the Generative Chakra spins at the slowest velocity.

In addition, we should not imagine that because we may be undergoing an awakening to, for example, the energies of the Generative Chakra, that no energies are moving in or being expressed through the other chakras. The individualizing process is about becoming *conscious* of what is occurring in our energy fields. It is all going on all the time, most of it without our conscious awareness.

To awaken to a certain phase of the process is like focusing the spotlight of our attention on it. When we do that, we increase the flow of energy in that phase of the process because our attention is held there. But we do not *cease* the flow of energy through the rest of our field or through our expression of other functions. Those functions may not be in the forefront of our consciousness, but they do not cease.

What Happens When the Release of the Creative Force Is Heightened?

In Chapter Two we talked about the urge to be of service, an expression of the energies of the Devotional Ray moving through the Generative Chakra and motivating us to action. That is a powerful and universal expression of creative energy, and it is fostered by society because it promotes the welfare of others.

Another way the force released in the Generative Chakra is experienced is as the urge to engage in sexual intercourse. The instinctive urge to procreate is registered as a strong and almost irresistible attraction to someone of the opposite gender. When that urge is still quite unconscious in the individual, the groups to which the individual belongs usually control that urge through the inculcation of moral values and taboos. Young men and women are encouraged to express the urge to procreate only in ways that conform to societal values and institutions. Some societies prohibit partnering with certain families or clans, ethnic groups and nationalities, or social or economic groupings. Nearly all societies prohibit copulation with close relatives. Age restrictions may be imposed. Or, parents may actually choose the individuals with whom a son or daughter will be allowed to procreate. These customs seek to perpetuate societal patterns and to ensure the healthy continuity of societal groups.

The forces associated with the Devotional Ray also motivate the development of certain skills that will enable us to serve others in more specifically creative ways. However, in the unconscious phase of the unfolding process, the building of family units is primary. People develop their skills in order to support their families, rather than to fulfill a creative urge. How they earn their living is not as important as their ability to provide that support.

When we begin to awaken, that is, to become conscious of the choices we are making, the creative urge of the Generative Chakra expands beyond the urge to procreate and to be of service to our families. We begin to feel an urge to make a larger contribution in the world. We are no longer content to restrict ourselves to the raising of a family.

It is at this stage that we begin to have an urge to pursue a career, or to develop particular gifts and give them life and expression in the world. Abundant, unrestricted energy is released in response to our conscious attention that can be utilized in any pursuit, whether in the arts, politics, business, education, religion, social reform, science, technology, sports, or whatever.

The flow of force through the Generative Chakra is augmented by our awareness of the motivating urge of the Devotional Ray, which increases both concentration and devotion. Though we might not know anything about our energetic structure or the energy of the Rays moving through us, we are nevertheless aware of *what we want to do.* We know we want to make a contribution with our lives, and we may be clear what career path we want to follow. These are the ways we identify the urge moving in us before we understand the cosmic forces at work.

When we have reached that level of awareness, *all* expressions of the Generative Chakra are amplified. Consequently, individuals who are awakening usually also have an unusually strong sexual urge. If their devotion is primarily to their career, not to the building of a family, their sexual relationships may represent more of a spillover of creative energy than an expression of devotion to the individuals with whom they engage.

This, I believe, explains the behavior of many men who have been outstanding in their specialized fields of expression and who have been promiscuous in their sexual behavior. The directing of so much energy through the Generative Chakra, due to their devotion to the pursuit of social reform, political office, business enterprises, artistic expression, religious service, athletic prowess, etc., can result in an unrestrained expression of sexual energy. They have more creative force available than their state of consciousness enables them to direct consciously. Thus, even married men with high morals may have extramarital affairs.

Women, on the other hand, tend to express their excess creative energy in nurturing activities. They devote themselves to taking care of spouse and children, making improvements around the home, and cooking and baking even though they have little time available beyond the requirements of their career. They may also nurture the growth of a business, or pursue artistic expression with devotion. Or such women may take in "stray" children or adults who need a home or a mentor, or give an inordinate amount of time and energy to emotionally needy people, or pour out their energy in volunteer service activities of various kinds.

Often these individuals earn the highest respect of their colleagues and of the public, in the case of famous men and women, for their contributions in their chosen field. Yet when the sexual indiscretions of men are revealed, people do not understand that apparent moral lapse. Usually women do not get exposed in the same way, but their families and close friends would be able to tell you of their excesses in the nurturing realm. And in the case of both men and women, our culture is becoming more aware of the costs of nurturing devotion when it gets out of balance. Excess in any expression can create chaos and havoc in body, psyche, home life and other relationships.

We need to recognize that these individuals are no longer under the control of their societal taboos, mores, and morals. If they were they would probably not have made the same creative strides in their chosen areas of pursuit because they would have focused on protecting and perpetuating what had already been brought into manifestation. This does not excuse their sexual indiscretions or obsessive nurturing, but it may help us to understand their dilemma, and in our own lives, it may help us to exercise more conscious and balanced self-control.

Are Sexual Energies Only for the Purpose of Procreation?

Sexual engaging is only one among the many creative expressions that are possible in the frequencies of the Generative Chakra. Sexual intercourse emerged in the unfolding process as an instinct to ensure the survival of the species. In most animals, the urge to procreate (that is, the arousal of sexual energies) arises only at certain times of the year in what we call the mating season. During that season, both males and females are instinctively programmed to mate in order to reproduce. Copulating is not something animals do for pleasure. They do it to discharge the energy that has arisen in them as part of a natural cycle.

Human beings have remnants of the instinctive urge to mate. In the spring, for example, many people feel a pronounced increase of interest in persons of the opposite sex. And in adolescence, the surge in hormones awakens a desire to engage in intercourse. However, humans are not attracted to one another *only* on the basis of the urge to procreate. In fact, that urge is not a predominant factor for most people, even in their sexual expression.

Humans have learned to use sexual engaging for many different purposes. Sometimes it is used to discharge the pressure of energy that has been called up but has not been used in another creative expression. Often sexual intercourse provides pure sensual enjoyment. It can express or strengthen deep emotional or spiritual ties. Or, it may serve to celebrate an experience that has been fulfilling on all levels. When the polarities of two individuals are properly aligned, sexual intercourse can actually recharge the two energetically, bringing their individual forces into balance and giving both partners new energy with which to go forth into the world. And the list could go on.

The introduction of birth control devices in the 20th century made it possible for increasing numbers of people, without risk of unwanted pregnancies, to expand their sexual expression far beyond the instinctual urge to procreate. Many taboos and societal strictures have fallen by the wayside as a result. Now that procreation is no longer the primary focus, monogamy is not as urgent and a marriage license has become less important. Many people today engage in numerous sexual liaisons, long-term intimacy without marriage is increasingly common, engaging sexually with people of the same sex is less of a taboo, and continuing sexual activity into the senior years is more commonplace.

These changes in the expression of sexual energies reflect the increase of conscious choice making that accompanies the individualizing process. As people become aware of their own urges in the Generative Chakra and are no longer governed solely by instinct, they often choose to ignore societal constraints.

However, this does not mean that they understand the significance of the increased creative force moving in them. Therefore their sexual expression does not necessarily support or enhance their process of awakening.

How Can We Consciously Direct Creative Energies?

In the Wisdom Tradition, aspirants were given guidance and instruction regarding sexual energies. They were taught to recognize them as an expression of the one universal creative force that has brought everything into being. That creative force is available to us as human beings so that we might become conscious co-creators in the universe. When the energies of the Generative Chakra are quickened, we awaken to this creative force and begin to make conscious choices about its expression.

If too much Generative Chakra energy is expended in sexual engaging, it can dissipate the urge to create in other ways and forms. Consequently, aspirants in the Wisdom Tradition were taught how to transmute the energies of the sexual urge into higher frequencies of expression. They were taught not to identify the arousal of the creative force with the physical body. Rather, they were to view it as the one cosmic creative force seeking to be expressed through them. The excitement thus aroused was lifted up, on the breath, and held high, out of the instinctual frequency range, until, in harmony with other chakra energies, the aspirant gave it conscious expression.

This was not to avoid all sexual intercourse. Rather, it was to free the aspirant from unconscious responses to instinctual urges so that the urge to create could be directed consciously into chosen avenues of expression.

The creative force was held sacred in the Wisdom Traditions. Aspirants were urged to give it expression, in harmony with the Devotional Ray, in ways that would serve the larger Will.

In the Generative Chakra, creative force is expressed whenever we bring anything into physical form. Giving birth to a new human is an obvious result of sexual engaging between male and female. However, it is only one of a multitude of expressions of creativity through this chakra. Each time a meal is made from scratch, a painting is painted, a book is published, a concert is given, a recording is made, clothing is manufactured, a letter is written and mailed, a presentation is made, a play is opened on stage, a song is written, a movie is released, a house is constructed – each time something new is brought into being, whether by one person or by a group of people who cooperate in the effort – creative force has been brought into form.

The urgency of the drive to create increases when the forces in the Generative Chakra are quickened during the awakening process. It almost demands that we contribute something to the world around us. These Generative Chakra contributions take the form of things that can be touched, heard, seen, tasted, or smelled. Earth energies predominate in these contributions. They are accessible to all humans. And the more awakened the individual is who creates, the more unique and beautiful the creation will be, and the more pleasure it will give to others who are developed enough to appreciate it.

Other creations through the Generative Chakra are not themselves tangible, but produce tangible results. For example, a creative person might bring a new educational program into being that, until it is embodied, is not a physical object. Yet, once the program is underway, many tangible results can be pointed to and experienced, not the least of which are the students who benefit from the program. Or, a businessman might bring a corporation into being which, in its legal form, is abstract and exists only on paper. However, once the activities of the corporation begin, countless tangible products may be brought into being.

The creative contribution of such individuals is not diminished by the delay in the appearance of tangible results.

How Does This Quickening of Force Promote the Individualizing Process?

The quickening of energies in the Generative Chakra is the first stage of the awakening process. We become conscious as individuals of how the universal forces are moving in our energy fields. During this first phase, we learn to make conscious choices about how to express our creative energies. We are no longer at the effect of instinctual urges that would send us out to pursue a mate with whom to procreate. Instead, we recognize the creative force as an urge to bring something new into manifestation, and we pursue avenues of expression for our talents, gifts, and personal interests.

For some, that creative expression might take the form of a family and children. If so, this is undertaken with conscious and unwavering devotion. For others, creativity might be expressed through a career in the arts, business, politics, religion, education, social work, etc., or through a leisure pursuit, such as volunteer work, writing, sculpting, painting, photography, etc. Such pursuits can be equal in intensity to raising a family. All can be expressions of the urge to serve the creative impulse with devotion.

In the metaphor of the House of Self, this is the stage of development when we begin to clean out the basement of the House of Self and to give it new order according to our growing understanding. We no longer feel constrained to conform to the groups by which we were raised. We begin to explore how to make this House of Self fully our own, an expression of our own unique constellation of the forces of the universe moving through us. Though we are still largely identified with our bodies and psyches, we begin to have a sense of self as utterly unique. We begin to think and feel, "This is who I am," and to know that we are not exactly like anyone else in our neighborhood.

> **Ways to Practice:**
> 1. **During your quiet time each morning,** spend about five minutes focusing your attention in the Generative Chakra. (Use the body to find the frequency. Hold your attention on the area of the reproductive organs.) As you inhale, direct the energy of the breath into the Generative Chakra. As you exhale, imagine that energy radiates out through the Generative Chakra throughout your entire field, giving you life force for the day's activities.

2. At the beginning of the day, set the intention to be aware of the Generative Chakra energies. When you are conscious of energy stirring there, think of it as creative force rather than as sexual arousal. Ask yourself what you want to bring into being with this creative force.

3. As you work on creative activities throughout the day, consciously breathe into the Generative Chakra and direct the creative force into what you are creating. This is any activity that brings something into being on the physical level. Do not restrict your definition of creativity to so-called "art" forms.

4. As you move through your days, observe yourself. Be conscious of your urges to create, to "do." What urges are yours and which ones belong to group psyches with which you have been identified?

4
Freedom to Direct Forces

The activation of more consciousness of self, which is the beginning of the awakening process, begins in the Generative Chakra rather than the Sacral Chakra. This is because the first phase of the awakening process takes place in the psyche, not in the autonomous field.[1] The frequencies of five of the seven energy centers correspond to the psyche: the Generative, Solar Plexus, Heart, Throat, and Third Eye Chakras, and the awakening begins with the Generative Chakra.

It is crucial to our understanding of the individualizing process that we grasp the symbolism that corresponds to this opening. ***Our awakening begins with our awareness of the creative force moving in the body.*** Generally speaking, the effect of this awakening is the sensation of a subtle vibration in the region of the sexual organs. Since most persons are not aware of neural stimulation in this region except when sexual energies are aroused, and since it is extremely rare that the individual is aware that an awakening is occurring in the Generative Chakra, this subtle vibration can create confusion.

---

[1]. See Chapter Twelve for a description of the autonomous field.

First of all, many people in Western cultures are raised with attitudes that disparage the physical body and sexual expression. For hundreds of years, religious teachings implied, or directly stated, that salvation could be attained only by denying or rising above physical desires and expressions. The vow of celibacy taken by most priests, nuns, and monks reinforced that assertion.

In addition, in the United States many church authorities, government officials, and even educators have been reluctant to support sex education, and those who have promoted sex education have often suffered the anger of parents who vehemently oppose anyone outside the home providing sexual guidance to their children. This is often because of their religious upbringing and their own feelings of inadequacy with regard to educating their children about their sexuality.

Sexual images are used to sell everything in our culture, from automobiles to life insurance. Yet a majority of adults are still embarrassed to speak of the generative organs in public or to acknowledge the beauty of the naked human body.

Such restrictions are not characteristic only of Western cultures. In many, if not most, cultures, to speak openly and frankly about a woman's sexual organs is simply not done. The female vagina, clitoris, and labia are seldom mentioned at all. When males refer to the female vagina or womb, they almost always use offensive slang terms.

This reluctance to name the reproductive organs is not just in relation to women. Around the world, dozens of euphemisms are used to speak of the male sexual organ, yet seldom do we hear the word *penis*.

The failure to speak openly and matter-of-factly

about sexual organs and the reproductive process has led many people to ignore their bodies when at all possible, as if it were better not to pay attention to them. Some people try to live outside of their bodies. Such attitudes make the appreciation of the sacredness of the creative force almost impossible.

What is worse is that because the urge to procreate has been denigrated and kept out of "polite conversation," the urge itself has often been repressed. This is like damming up water. The pressure that builds is enormous and when the creative force finally breaks out, it is often destructive rather than creative. Much physical violence is almost certainly due to repressed Generative Chakra energies, and many sexual expressions that are frowned on by the majority of people, such as a fascination with pornography or sado-masochistic expression, are actually a reflection of the general denial of sexual urges.

When appreciation of the beauty of the human body cannot be expressed openly, the natural urge to express oneself sexually goes underground and people pay to see photographs of the pleasure they deny themselves in their ordinary lives. All sexual abuse, including the rape of small children, is surely the release of sexual energy that could no longer be held back. It takes unacceptable forms because the energy itself is deemed unacceptable by so many group psyches.

In addition, the repression of the urge to procreate often leads to the development of sexual addictions. When we do not allow ourselves to enjoy sexual intercourse fully, the urge to engage sexually can become almost insatiable. It is not possible for that urge to be completely satisfied as long as it is not viewed as the most sacred of all energies.

The creative force that humans experience as the urge to procreate is the primal expression of the Original One. It brought our entire cosmos into manifestation. This creative force is both the beginning (the alpha) and the end (the omega) of all that is. When it arises in us, asking for release, it is an invitation to share the creative work of Self-discovery and Self-expression set in motion by the Original One. Instead of responding with denial and repression, we need to learn to respond with awe, wonder, and an enormous sense of privilege that we can give that force conscious expression.

What Symbols Are Commonly Used for the Quickening of This Creative Urge in the Generative Chakra?

It is important to understand that our awakening begins with a quickening of the forces in the Generative Chakra because the symbolism used in the Wisdom Teachings can only be understood in that light.

The sacred stories about enlightened beings like Jesus and Gautama Buddha begin, almost without exception, with a divine birth. This symbolism is difficult to grasp if we have been raised to denigrate life in the body and the procreative act that results in a birth.

In the story of Jesus' life, for example, an angel announced his conception, angelic hosts announced his birth, he was born in a manger among the animals, and wise men from the East paid homage to him as an infant. What do these symbols mean?

The angel's appearance to Mary telling her that she would give birth to a son is symbolic of an intuitive registry by one who is about to begin the individualizing process. Many of us have had a similar intuition, even though we may not have spoken of it as the visitation of an angel. Nevertheless, we have felt strongly that something new and magnificent was about to begin for us. If we had known the symbolism taught in the Wisdom Traditions, we might have recognized that we were awakening to a conscious awareness of who we really are, namely, incarnations of the divine.

The heralding of Jesus' birth by hosts of angels who appeared to shepherds watching their flocks in the fields at night is symbolic of the first recognition by the rational mind that something extraordinary has occurred. Sheep are a symbol for thoughts that, unless shepherded, wander aimlessly and get lost. Part of our development is learning to discipline our thoughts in order to focus our awareness. When the awareness comes "in the night" of our unconscious functioning that we are somehow "new" even though nothing external appears to have changed, we are at a second level of recognition of the awakening in the generative energies.

The visit by the wise men of the East paying homage to the Christ child is symbolic of a third level of our emerging understanding of the transformation occurring in the Generative Chakra. The wise men represent the wisdom to recognize that we are divine energy expressed in newborn awareness.

And what does being born in a manger among the animals symbolize? This is so important for the cultures in which sexuality is denied in many ways. Consciousness of our divinity awakens first *in the body*, in the frequencies that are closer to the animals than to the angels. As humans, we have unfolded from within the overall cosmic process. We emerged out of the animal field of consciousness. When we become *aware* of the powerful creative force moving in us, and urges to pursue many different creative activities and expressions begin to stir, we fulfill the promise of the entire evolutionary process, including the faculties developed in the animal field. We begin to recognize that we are the divine force incarnate, and that is a startling awareness to most human beings.

The awakening in the Generative Chakra usually goes unacknowledged by the personality at the time it is occurring. Even in the story of Jesus' birth there is no indication that there was a wide public awareness that something extraordinary had occurred. People in the neighborhood didn't come running to see him. Only the wise men from the East, symbolizing our higher spiritual faculties, and the shepherds, representing the trained rational faculties, knew something truly sacred had occurred.

The symbolism of the divine birth is often true to the experience of even the most ordinary person, but without mental understanding (the trained rational faculties), it takes a long time to recognize the significance of the generative awakening. Sometimes we feel as if a great change is taking place. We feel a surge of creativity that seems to demand that we "do" something even if we aren't able to discover readily what the "something" is. Sometimes we even feel "chosen," as if God or the Universe has set us apart to do a great work. Often Generative Chakra awakenings are accompanied by an increase in sexual appetite.

These are some of the signs of the first phase of the awakening process even when we have no conscious awareness of it. But many don't notice the subtle changes until other chakras begin to open.

How Do We Clean House in the Basement?

Often our first energetic self-awareness is that all is not well in the way we are living in and through the body. The recognition that some serious changes need to be made, beginning with some house cleaning, may indicate that a quickening has occurred. We may have developed addictions to food, drugs, alcohol, tobacco, and/or sex. If so, we need to free ourselves of those addictions before we can awaken further.

It is also possible that we are not healthy of body. We may need to heal some condition of dis-ease that has arisen, or to build our strength and balance through a program of physical stretches and exercise. Perhaps we need to lose weight or to eat in a more balanced and healthy way. We may need to learn to love the body and to live more fully in it and through it. Dance, sports, massage, and other sensually pleasureful activities, including physical lovemaking, may help us to rediscover how delightful it is to be physically alive.

In these ways and others, we awaken to the forces moving through the Generative Chakra, which are the Devotional Ray activating in us the urge to serve the creative impulse through our individual, embodied expression. A natural response to this urge is the awareness that we need to metaphorically clean the basement of the house of self. That is, we need to gain conscious jurisdiction over the instinctive urges that have governed the life of the body. We need to identify group patterns that have held sway over us, and we need to free ourselves of unconscious patterns that interfere with our conscious functioning through the body.

Imagine discovering that the divine consciousness is alive in our bodies. Imagine living with a feel-

ing of reverence for the creative force moving in us. Imagine discovering that through our physical activities, we are giving expression to the primal urge to know Self.

Such feelings and discoveries are evidence that the psyche is awakening to the potential represented by the Generative Chakra.

The specific activities that accompany this first phase of awakening depend entirely on the development of our psyches up to that point. If in our objective state of consciousness we have cultivated qualities in the Generative Chakra that will support our unfolding in this new phase of awakening, we will have a relatively easy time with this phase of the awakening. If, on the other hand, we have developed qualities and habits that will keep us bound in slavery to group psyches and subconscious urges, we will have some hard work to do to free ourselves. Just freeing ourselves of societal attitudes toward sexuality takes considerable conscious attention for most of us.

What Is The Lunar Cycle?

The awakening of the psyche in the Generative Chakra is the beginning of the first phase of the individualizing process. *It is the beginning of recognizing that cosmic forces are moving through us and that we can learn to control and direct those forces with our conscious attention.*

In the Wisdom Teachings, these initial phases of the process of awakening are often referred to as the **Lunar Cycle** because we are becoming conscious of the Real Self through its *reflection* in the psyche. Just as the moon shines by reflecting the light of the sun, so

Freedom to Direct Forces 69

the psyche functions by reflection. At first it reflects the consciousness of the groups to which we belong. Then in the course of the awakening process it turns within to reflect the light of consciousness of the Real Self. This may account for the reversal of the bodies (turning inside out) mentioned earlier, at the bottom of page 17. [See also Illustrations #s 3 & 4.]

As previously mentioned, in the energetic structure of the individual five chakras belong to the psyche: the Generative, Solar Plexus, Heart, Throat, and Third Eye chakras. The initial awakening to the energy world, also sometimes called the First Crossing, takes place through these five centers. As we become aware of the forces moving through these chakras, we discover that we can have conscious control over them, and we begin to practice identifying the motivating forces moving through us and consciously directing the energy into expressions that are aligned with our conscious intentions.

In our consciousness we are still identified with the body and personality, yet we have developed the capacity to observe and direct the personality. Thus we are Self-conscious at a new level.

Another term used in the Wisdom Teachings to describe the first phase of awakening is the **Baptism by Water**. Ancient symbolism has long associated the psyche with water. Consequently, the story of Jesus going to John the Baptist to be immersed in the waters of the Jordan river was a symbolic representation of the need of the newly born consciousness of Self (which occurred in the Generative Chakra) to be lifted up through the other four chakras of the psyche. The new awareness of Self has to be immersed in the waters and then lifted out of them. We will speak more about this process of lifting the consciousness by guiding and directing the energies of the chakras as we proceed in our description of the awakening.

A third representation of this phase of the individualizing process is the familiar sign used by the medical profession and other healers, namely, **the staff of Hermes, or the Caduceus.** [Illustration #9.] The staff itself is referred to in the Old Testament as the rod that Moses used in the wilderness to strike the rock (the sleeping consciousness of the Self) and bring forth water (the psyche). The rod symbolizes the sacral-conarial axis (the invisible lines of force flowing between the Crown Chakra and the Sacral Chakra) around which the web of the autonomous field is woven.[2] The sacral-conarial axis is the fundamental core of an individual's energetic structure. It is this rod or staff that "comforts" the one undergoing birth into a physical body (which, in the Wisdom Teachings, is the "shadow of death" referred to in the 23rd Psalm) because it maintains the unbreakable connection with the cosmic forces, or the Real Self. More about this in Chapter Twelve below.

Around the staff of Hermes are intertwined two serpents, one moving clockwise and the other counterclockwise. These are the polarized expressions of the one creative force. They are called the Ida and Pingala forces in Sanskrit. In Chinese philosophy they are termed the Yin and the Yang. This interaction between the polarities of the creative force works to awaken the psyche to its own energetic functioning, since nothing can be brought into manifestation except by these two polarities working together in union.

---

2. See Chapter Twelve.

The Caduceus

Illustration #9

As the yin and yang forces, or the ida-pingala, begin their ascent around the central axis of the individual's energy field,[3] the energies of the psyche are stirred up into the heightened activity that we are calling a quickening or an awakening. That increased activity brings awareness of habits and qualities developed in the psyche that will have to be expurgated or transmuted before the newly emerging consciousness of Self can be lifted up to the next level.

For example, during the early stages of our development it is perfectly normal to be self-centered, looking out for our own well-being above that of all others, in response to the instinctive urge to self-preservation. However, as we begin to awaken, other urges take precedence. We develop a feeling of responsibility to and for others in response to the urge to be of service, and self-centeredness begins to fade. If there are habit patterns and values that represent the earlier urge to self-preservation, those will need to be transformed so that we can be responsive to the new, higher-frequency motivation.

Certain qualities in our fields were developed under the influence of group psyches. Some examples might be provincialism, racial and ethnic prejudice, distrust of foreigners, intolerance, isolation, and narrow-mindedness. These and many others will have to be let go of or transmuted into less insular attitudes and values.

Once the cleaning out of habits and qualities begins, major changes often take place in relationships. Friends with whom we have shared for years may fall out of our lives, or we may find that we no longer enjoy the company of those with whom we used to spend a lot

---

3. See description on pages 78 & 79 below.

Freedom to Direct Forces 73

of time. The shift of frequencies in our energy fields results in a lack of resonance with old associates and requires that we open to new companions who share our new state of development.

Sexual expression also changes. The instinctive sexual urge gradually weakens and we find that we are no longer aroused by the same visual images and tactile stimulation. Instead, we respond more readily to those with whom we are in frequency resonance. This can be disruptive to long standing relationships when only one partner awakens and the other remains in the objective state of consciousness.

It is often at this stage, when we are seeking companionship, that we find our way to study groups or classes where we not only meet others who are undergoing the same openings, but where we begin to get instruction that helps us to understand the process of awakening.

Ways to Practice:
Take time to notice what has been changing in your life.

1. What physical habits and preferences have changed? What are you consciously choosing by way of diet, exercise, and physical relationships that represent a new sensitivity and awareness? What addictions have you overcome?

74 THE HOUSE OF SELF

2. What has changed in the way you feel about your body and your sexuality?

3. What new creative activities are you engaged in? What old activities have you let go of?

4. What former relationships have fallen out of your life? What new relationships have entered?

5. **What more do you feel needs to change** to bring yourself into alignment with your current state of consciousness?

6. How can you allow yourself to express more creatively through your body? In dance, athletics, martial arts, or ???

Notes:

The Guest House

This being human is a guest house.
Every morning a new arrival.

A joy, a depression, a meanness,
some momentary awareness comes
as an unexpected visitor.

Welcome and entertain them all!
Even if they're a crowd of sorrows,
who violently sweep your house
empty of its furniture,
still, treat each guest honorably.
He may be clearing you out
for some new delight.

The dark thought, the shame, the malice,
meet them at the door laughing,
and invite them in.

Be grateful for whoever comes,
because each has been sent
as a guide from beyond.

– Rumi

5
Learning How to Feel

The individualizing process is one phase of the overall cosmic process of unfolding. Consequently, the awakening of a conscious awareness of our energetic structure would take place in us whether or not we had a mental overview of that structure. However, as students of the Wisdom, we have the opportunity to consciously cooperate with the cosmic process. By learning about the forces at work in and through us, we can learn to identify those forces as they manifest in our daily experience. Having identified them, we can learn how to direct the energy to enhance our further awakening.

It is important for us to recognize that *what we are not conscious of motivates our actions, feelings, and thoughts without any conscious control or direction on our part. But what we are conscious of we can learn to master.* Therefore, we study and practice the arts of consciousness.

In previous chapters, we have looked at the beginning of this process of awakening in the Generative Chakra. In our metaphor of the House of Self, the awakening begins in the basement. Only after considerable clearing out and reordering of the contents of the basement do we begin to notice stirrings in the Solar Plexus Chakra. At that point our attention shifts and we, so to speak, climb the stairs out of the basement and focus our awareness on the first floor of the House of Self.

There is no way to predict how long the quickening of the generative energies will take in any given individual's life because so many factors are in play. If the individual has gone through the awakening process in past incarnations, the stages will be repeated in this one much more rapidly. On the other hand, if the early years of building a new psyche have resulted in deep wounds, severe distortions of perception, addictive patterns, etc., more time may be required to get free before the individual can move on to the next stage of the process.

What is important is that we trust the process and not try to rush it. If there is cleansing of the psyche that needs to be accomplished in the Generative Chakra in relation to wounds, addictive patterns, distorted perceptions of the body, etc., we can devote ourselves to that work without holding ourselves back as we grow in other areas. The work of cleansing on one level may overlap with the opening and cleansing work of other chakra levels. In fact, sometimes patterns in the psyche involve energies from several chakras and thus work needs to be done on all those levels to complete the process. In other words, we might end up working alternately between the basement and the first floor of the House of Self, and even on the second floor. We will speak more about this cleansing process in the chapter that follows.

As the process of awakening occurs in us, the yin and yang forces spiral around the energetic axis of our fields, moving up through the frequency bands of the five chakras of the psyche. [See Illustration #9.] They stir and activate those chakra energies so that the way can be made clear for what the Greeks called the Christos power, or what in Sanskrit is called the Kundalini, to travel from the Sacral Chakra through the five centers of the psyche and into the Crown Chakra where the yin and yang unite, completing the individualizing process. The lunar phase of the awakening clears the way for a higher-frequency power to function through us. It is to this clearing process that the Biblical phrase "Make straight the way of the Lord" refers.

In the metaphor of the House of Self, the lunar phase of the individualizing process is like rewiring the house to be able to bring in high voltage electrical currents without blowing any circuits. Not only do our nervous systems need to be prepared for the increased power that the Christos will release in us, but also every other organ in the body needs to be recalibrated.

It is important to state that *we* are not responsible for the rewiring of the House of Self. The creative force itself, through the agency of these yin-yang polarities, does the work. However, we can *facilitate* the work by cooperating with it rather than resisting it. It is as if the yin and yang energies are electricians who come into the House of Self and begin to change the wiring, to recalibrate all the appliances (organs) that plug into the current, and to test out the new capacity of the electrical system to see if it is working properly. We, as residents in the house, are conscious of the activity but do not interfere with it. We leave it to the experts, even if sometimes we are frightened or perplexed by the effects of their work. In fact, we may facilitate their work by moving things out of their way, namely, unproductive patterns like worrying and obsessing about what we don't understand.

I recall when the rewiring process was going on in my House of Self. The "electricians" had worked on my elbows, my knees, and my forehead. Then suddenly "they" went to work with great intensity on the soles of my feet. I got out of bed one morning and felt like I had stepped onto a bed of hot coals. I let out a scream of pain and sat down again on the bed. Then with utmost consciousness, I gingerly stepped on my feet. Fire! Intense burning! My objective mind screamed, "Call the doctor!"

However, my knowing was that the doctor would find nothing wrong. The process continued for days. I finally went to a doctor, all the while knowing he could do nothing for me. In confirmation of my knowing, he said he could find nothing that would cause the burning. I went home, my objective mind satisfied, and simply waited out the process. One day it was finished and the force moved on to my shoulders.

Although we are not responsible for the changes that occur in the energetic structure of the House of Self, we can cooperate with the process. As mentioned in earlier chapters, simply by observing the energies moving in the Generative Chakra, reflected in our bodies, we help to free ourselves from old habit patterns. We can learn to transmute qualities that no longer serve us. We can focus our attention in the Generative Chakra energies (in the region of the reproductive organs in the body) and align our breathing, on the inhale, with receiving the forces from the cosmos around us and directing them, on the exhale, into our intentional activities. As we get good at that alignment and at sensing how to direct the energy, we can then learn to lift the forces from the Generative Chakra into the Solar Plexus, and from the Solar Plexus into the Heart Chakra. In all those ways we cooperate consciously with what is occurring naturally.

How Do We Direct the Force of Desire?

As the yin and yang energies spiral around the sacral-conarial axis, moving from the Generative Chakra to the Solar Plexus Chakra, we also move out of the frequencies in which the earth element predominates into frequencies in which the element of water prevails. In the earth energies, we relate to all things tangible. In the psychic waters we move to the intangible realm of emotions, which are often reflected in the body but are otherwise inaccessible to the five senses. Like the element of earth, the element of water tends to pull energies downward into lower frequencies and inward to the more personal and subjective realms.

In the western Wisdom Tradition, as in many other symbol systems, water is used to represent the emotions. That is because the emotions are changeable, like water, responding to external forces. When there is conflict of some kind, the waters of the psyche become turbulent. When all is going well in our lives, the emotions become placid like a still lake. But in the depths of the waters, many secret fears may be hidden. Wounds, and the pains accompanying them, are often buried there. And unfulfilled desires await our discovery.

In this lunar phase of the awakening process, we discover there are deep and powerful forces at work in the psyche, experienced by us as desire. These forces ripple throughout our fields as feeling responses to the expression of desire, its frustration or its fulfillment.

Some of the desires that work in us unconsciously before this awakening process begins are "I want to be accepted by others," "I want to be liked," "I want to be loved." There is nothing wrong with these desires. In fact, their fulfillment is essential to our emotional health and well being, so that we feel safe in our social environment and have feelings of self-worth. However, when those desires are thwarted, we sometimes develop compensatory desires, such as the desire to control others, the desire to hurt others, or the desire to rebel. Those desires can be very powerful. However, they work against our self-interest and eventually turn to bitterness, envy, and even self-hatred.

During the process of socialization, most of us were taught that we could not have everything we wanted. Sometimes as a way of restraining our desires authority figures told us not to be "selfish." They may have told us to put others first, or at least to share with others. Or they may have said it was not appropriate to want a given something because of our race, religion, nationality, ethnic group, gender, age, or socio-economic status. Numerous reasons were given to justify their need to have us conform to societal guidelines, both spoken and implied.

Imagine what happens when all those repressed desires, many never even allowed to surface into consciousness, are stirred up by the dynamism of the yin-yang forces. Not only is internal conflict likely to arise as we try to maintain control over desires we were taught were "bad," but also our relationships are likely to be thrown into upheaval. People will be offended and hurt as we pursue our desires with the fierceness of a warrior. They will say, "This is not like you," or

"What has happened to you?" Some will feel betrayed, others abandoned.

Women, for example, are often taught to put other people's needs before their own. In the interest of serving others, they set aside their own desires for a career. When the yin and yang currents begin to stir the waters of the Solar Plexus, such women may assert themselves, saying, "I'm going back to college or back to work." Husbands and children may not understand this sudden unrest. They may feel their own lives are being disrupted and they may resent that. Or they may feel abandoned. When the quickening of the Solar Plexus energies has begun, however, the women are not likely to retreat. They may even become fiercer in their pursuits when others try to bring them back into conformity.

Or a man may have put aside his desire for adventure and experimentation in order to take a job that would support a wife and family. If, some years later, the rising polar forces stir the waters of the Solar Plexus, he may suddenly declare that he is quitting his job in order to sail around the world for a year. To his wife and family this declaration may seem irrational, and they may feel their own well-being is threatened, but the husband may plunge ahead without regard to the consequences.

In spite of the seeming dangers encountered during this phase of our awakening, we develop our willingness to explore all those hidden motivations and desires that we have kept in the shadow of our awareness.

Many desires are connected with or related to urges moving in the Generative Chakra. For example, if sexual urges have been repressed, the motivating force may have moved up in frequency to the Solar

Plexus where strong *desires* for sexual expression may have taken form. This goes beyond the instinctual urge to procreate or even the arousal of sexual attraction. The *desire* to have sex is often accompanied by mental images of objects of desire and fantasies about sexual engaging. These picture images make it impossible to satisfy the sexual urge through physical intercourse. Now the *desire* must be satisfied as well, and that means that somehow the picture images need to be fulfilled. Many marriages begin to fall apart when one or another partner has a desire that the spouse cannot satisfy because he or she doesn't fit the image.

Or, if urges to pursue a career have been frustrated in the generative wave band of frequencies, a deep *desire to succeed* may have formed in Solar Plexus energies. Again, this desire will be sustained with images and definitions of success that may be inflated and exaggerated. Such a person may make a lot of money, earn the respect of colleagues, be given promotions, and even become famous. But if her *images* are not fulfilled, she may still not feel successful.

If a given relationship failed, a *strong desire* to find a lasting relationship may have been awakened in response. This desire can cause one to cling to partners, thus driving them away. Or, the desire can give birth to the fear that no relationship will ever be lasting, and the fear can give birth to jealousy of the partner, suspicions about the partner's activities or intentions, accusations of unfaithfulness, and other destructive behaviors and emotions.

In these and many other cases, identifying the motivating urges becomes more complex. A **desire** may mask an urge to pursue something in generative energies. That urge is yang, whereas desire tends to be yin. Longing for something in the solar plexus may not give us satisfaction if the urge is really to pursue in yang energy. In fact, desire can actually be self-defeating if we spend our energies in the yin polarity, waiting for someone or something else to fulfill them, rather than activating yang initiative to get what we want.

For instance, we may *desire* sexual fulfillment, but we wait for the object of our desire to come to us rather than making our needs and wants known to the one beside us who wants to give us love. Or we want a successful career, but we wait for some ultimate image of success rather than rejoicing in the realization of the efforts we have already put forth. Or we want a lasting relationship, but we do not give expression to qualities and behaviors that would cause our relationships to last. Instead, we look to our partners to fulfill our desire and fear they will not do so.

Desire is a powerful motivating force that, like steam, needs to be directed into the engine of action or thought. Then it provides power for the activity that will eventually bring fulfillment of the desire. If it is not partnered with some yang expression, however, the force builds up until it explodes in frustration. Then it often reverses polarity and becomes a demand, which attempts to force another to grant what we have not learned to create for ourselves.

How Do Feelings Serve Us?

The energies of the Solar Plexus Chakra are associated with our digestive organs because it is in those energies that we digest and integrate our life experiences. To digest them, we must first *feel* them. **Feelings** *are the faculty of consciousness with which we determine whether or not something pleases us.* Though this is not the only function of feelings, it is their primary function when we are still relatively unconscious.

With our physical senses we see, touch, smell, and taste food that we ingest. We might turn aside food based on the registry of any of these senses: it's too green/black, too hard/soft, too rancid/sour, etc. In the Solar Plexus we make similar assessments of our life experiences through our feelings or emotional sensitivity. If something doesn't *feel good* to us, we are reluctant to digest it.

What does it mean to digest a life experience? By processing an experience through our feelings, we come to know it thoroughly. To integrate an experience is like digesting food. The experience must be broken down into its components. Some will be used to strengthen us and others will be discarded just as waste is released from the body.

It is as if we place the experience in a large pot full of water, which is held in the Solar Plexus. As we breathe into the feelings, the breath gives oxygen to the fire of feeling beneath the pot and in time the water begins to boil. The feeling both under and in the pot coaxes out the flavor of the experience and we begin to smell it and eventually to taste it. Only when it is completely cooked can we swallow and digest the whole event, integrating it into the way we know ourselves.

Suppose the experience was that your father died when you were ten years old. When you turn your attention to that event, you feel paralyzed with fear. You go numb and are unable to feel or to remember what happened that day and in the weeks that followed.

To digest and integrate the experience, you would

Learning How to Feel 87

place the memory in the Solar Plexus pot. Suppose you remember seeing your mother come into your room. You remember *knowing* she was going to tell you that your father was dead.

It is the image of your mother coming through your bedroom door that you will place in the pot. Then, without letting the image out of your inner sight, you will begin to breathe consciously into the fire beneath it, inviting it to show you what you need (and needed) to know. You keep breathing deeply and slowly until the experience begins to come to life in you (the water begins to boil) and the various components of the event begin to make themselves known to you. You keep breathing even if strong feelings come up, moving the energy on through and releasing it, like steam lifting off the boiling water.

Perhaps the fear comes forth first. After time, anger rises to the surface, and as you boil the anger, feeding breath into it, you realize that your mother didn't tell you how sick your father was and you didn't get to see him in those last days. After a time of feeling the anger, perhaps profound loss comes up as you let yourself feel that your father really is dead and you will *never* see him again.

Then a series of feelings may follow – laughter at how happy you were when your father played with you, tenderness as you imagine how ill he must have been those last months, regrets that you never told him how much you loved him, pride when you remember how he bragged about you to his friends, disappointment at how much you missed by his early death, anger that he was taken from you, and so forth.

You don't quit breathing until all the feelings have been cooked out of the experience. You will feel spent.

You will sigh. The sigh is a spontaneous expression of your acceptance that your father is dead.

In the days that follow you will begin to harvest one awareness after another of what you learned from your father, what his legacy is in your life, and what you learned from his death. That experience is now yours and you have integrated it into your knowledge of yourself.

Painful experiences are often difficult to digest. We don't like to experience physical pain, but we often seek to avoid emotional pain even more vigorously. However, just as undigested food can make us physically ill, so painful experiences that are never lived through, felt, and integrated can cause emotional disorders as well as physical illness.

An important part of the process of awakening on the Solar Plexus level, then, is to bring into consciousness painful experiences from the past that have never been integrated. Psychotherapy can be very helpful in this regard, as can journaling and various therapeutic support groups. Emotional pain can usually be lived through when we feel safe and lovingly supported by caring persons.

In the metaphor of the House of Self it is as though for the first time we take a look at the furniture and decoration of the ground floor of the house that was built for us by our relatives with the help of others in the community. We find that contributions to our growth were not always pleasing to us and we may have tried to ignore them. But to function consciously in the Solar Plexus frequencies, we must now look at everything that is there, feel what we feel, let go of what no longer serves us, and recognize any desires that have still not been filled. It is our personal responsibility to find ways to satisfy those desires so that we can move on to higher frequencies within the Solar Plexus Chakra.

How Can We Recognize The Opening of the Solar Plexus?

Usually the opening of the Solar Plexus is accompanied by an increased sensitivity to the events and circumstances in which we are living. Many people find it almost impossible to be in the presence of emotional conflict when the Solar Plexus begins to open. People often report feeling "sick to their stomach" when in the presence of arguments or expressions of hostility.

The Ray that is channeling energy through the Solar Plexus Chakra is called **Harmony.** It motivates us to find ways to bridge gaps of difference between people and points of view and to mediate amidst conflict, pain, and struggle. Those who grow up in families where arguing and fighting are a predominant mode of communication often find that this urge is strong in them. They seek stability in their lives by helping to resolve conflict.

The Harmony Ray also makes us particularly sensitive to the kind of harmony that manifests as beauty. It stimulates the creative energy in us to bring forth expressions of beauty through rhythm, sound, and color. Responding to this urge, we can be motivated to help people communicate better so that they are not in constant conflict and/or we can follow the impulse to contribute to harmony on the interpersonal level by creating a beautiful environment for living and becoming. With works of art, beautiful music, fragrances that enhance relaxation and focus, fine food, and order and balance in the use of space and the placement of furnishings, the energies of the Solar Plexus will tend to seek a matching harmony and inner peace.

Many who are beginning to respond to the Harmony Ray experience the reflection of emotional disharmony on the physical level. They may have acute gas attacks, develop ulcers or irritable bowel syndrome, experience acid reflux, or in other ways find that their digestive processes have gone awry. Going to a medical doctor may not help if the difficulty is in their work place, in their home, or in a relationship. The heightened sensitivity to conflict may require that they find solace on the emotional level before the physical symptoms disappear.

The quickening of the forces in the Solar Plexus sometimes causes a stirring of energies that are mistaken for anxiety. By breathing into those energies and breathing out through the Solar Plexus, we can learn to release more force through the Solar Plexus and thus alleviate that pressure.

Another sensation that often accompanies the Solar Plexus opening is a pulsing, or thumping, that feels similar to a heartbeat only it is in the region of the stomach rather than in the chest. Sometimes that pulse can be very strong, seeming to shake the energy field like a drum beating from within. Again, it is helpful to breathe into that strong pulsing of energy and then breathe out through it, directing it into the larger field of energy around us so that we learn to utilize more force in the Solar Plexus.

During this activation of the forces in the Solar Plexus, many people find it necessary to be very selective about what they read, see, and listen to. Some stop reading the daily newspaper and watching the news on

Learning How to Feel 91

television so that they are not exposed to the violence that occurs daily throughout the world. Some will not be able to go to movies that depict violence or emotional trauma. And many will not be able to listen to friends and family talk about their problems or report their painful experiences. When exposed to disharmony over which they have no control, these people suffer unduly, taking on the effects of the disharmony without the power to resolve it.

An awareness of rapports is especially helpful during this phase of the awakening process. We establish rapport with persons with whom we have qualities and experiences in common. We feel drawn to those persons, sometimes feeling in harmony with them, other times feeling sympathy for them. What we experience consciously ("I feel incredibly attracted to this person," or "I identify with him because I have had the same problem," etc.) is like a floodgate. When we open to the one with whom we experience a rapport, the entire content of their consciousness floods in. That can create difficulties for us.

In this first phase of awakening, most of us continue to think objectively. That is, we think of ourselves as separate entities in a world of discrete objects and persons. We do not yet realize that we are living in a psychic ocean and that we function by registering frequencies. Consequently, when the feelings, thoughts, desires, and experiences of the one with whom we are in rapport flood into our consciousness, we think all the contents of his psyche are ours. They seem to be "in" us, so they must belong to us. Or so we think. Thus we can be overwhelmed by the feelings, thoughts, desires, and experiences and not know how to respond to them.

It is important that we learn to discriminate between different frequencies and the qualities that can be loaded onto them. It is important for us to learn to guide and direct our own forces so that we don't get them mixed up with the energies of others. And it is important to learn how to redirect and lift our own forces into higher frequencies and chakras when we want to free ourselves from influences in the Solar Plexus or Generative Chakras.

All of this learning comes with great difficulty if it is done only through trial and error. That is why it is helpful to find a teacher and/or a study group in which we can learn about the process of awakening once we have entered into that process ourselves.

Mars (and Pluto) in Scorpio

In esoteric astrology, **Scorpio** is the astrological sign utilized to represent the nature of the forces to be dealt with in the **Solar Plexus Chakra**. Scorpio is a water sign in astrology, and symbolically it points to the deep and powerful forces at work in the psyche, experienced by us as desire, and rippling throughout our fields as feeling responses to the expression of desire, its frustration or its fulfillment. In fact, the key words associated with the sign of Scorpio are "**I desire.**"

The planet **Mars in the sign of Scorpio** represents those forces when they are heightened by the infusion of more yin and yang force. **Mars** energy is powerful, fiery, and often stirs up conflict. For that reason Mars has been associated with the Warrior who fearlessly goes into battle to pursue what he desires. We can see how the energies of the Generative Chakra (symbolized by Jupiter in Sagittarius), in which the urge to pursue with devotion and passion is paramount, combined with the desires buried in the waters of the Solar Plexus (symbolized by **Scorpio**) might be very disruptive in a person's life when activated by the rising forces of yin and yang.

In 1930 the ninth planet in our Solar System was discovered. It was named **Pluto** and was assigned to share rulership of Scorpio with the planet Mars. Pluto was the god of the underworld in Roman mythology (called Hades in Greek mythology).

The discovery of this planet in the 20th century corresponded with the growing public awareness of the work in depth psychology launched by Freud and Jung. Perhaps it was the karmic responsibility of those who lived in the 20th century to dig deep in the waters of the psyche to gain new understanding of the subconscious urges, especially the need to exercise power or control that seems to rule in personal, national and international life and affairs.

The discovery of Pluto also heralded the onset of the Aquarian Age toward the end of the 20th Century and the unleashing of forces of deep transformation that would bring about great change in the new millennium.

Pluto is often considered a higher octave of Mars and is similarly powerful and penetrating, but on an unconscious and psychological level. It represents our willingness to explore all those hidden motivations and desires that we have kept in the shadow of our awareness. For those undergoing the process of awakening, the opportunities to plumb the depths of the waters of the psyche are greater since the discovery of Pluto, and the transformation of personalities is more intense and all-encompassing.

Ways to Practice:
1. **Sit quietly** with your feet on the floor and your spine erect. **Focus on the area of the navel,** holding the process of digestion in your awareness. **Consciously breathe in,** drawing energy up through the soles of your feet. Be aware that these are predominantly earth energies. Draw them up into the Solar

Plexus and breathe out through the Solar Plexus, dissolving the earth energies in water. Continue this practice until lifting the energies from the earth to the Solar Plexus is effortless.

2. During your quiet time each morning, breathe into the Solar Plexus and out through the Solar Plexus. Pay close attention to what you experience. See if you can begin to identify the quality of Solar Plexus energies without labeling a given feeling or emotion.

3. Choose an experience from the past about which you still have strong feelings. Call to mind the event that precipitated the feelings. Place it in a metaphorical pot on the stove of the Solar Plexus, holding it in your belly while you breathe into it. With each breath, feel the fire growing hotter. Hold the image of the event constant. Don't let it slip away. When feelings begin to arise, breathe into them. Feel them deeply, intensely. If memories from the event itself become clearer, keep holding them in the Solar Plexus and breathing into the fire underneath them until feelings arise. Continue the process, even if it takes days or weeks in increments of ten to fifteen minutes, until no more feelings arise and you feel finished. Often a deep and spontaneous sigh signals the end of the process.

4. Watch yourself in your interactions with others to see if you have established a rapport with anyone. In a rapport you lose your sense of boundaries and can no longer tell what feelings are yours and what feelings belong to the other. When you identify a rapport, take time to pull your energy back from this person and draw a mental boundary around your field to protect yourself from the further blending of your energies with the other. Develop a feeling of being a distinct individual from this other person. Identify what feelings *you* have that are different from those of the other.

5. In all circumstances, allow yourself to feel your feelings. Breathe into the Solar Plexus and give energy to those feelings. Let them inform you as to what *you* want in that circumstance.

Notes:

Last Night As I Was Sleeping

Last night as I was sleeping,
I dreamt — marvelous error! —
that a spring was breaking
out in my heart.
I said: Along which secret aqueduct,
Oh water, are you coming to me,
water of a new life
that I have never drunk?

Last night as I was sleeping,
I dreamt — marvelous error! —
that I had a beehive
here inside my heart.
And the golden bees
were making white combs
and sweet honey
from my old failures.

Last night as I was sleeping,
I dreamt — marvelous error! —
that a fiery sun was giving
light inside my heart.
It was fiery because I felt
warmth as from a hearth,
and sun because it gave light
and brought tears to my eyes.

Last night as I slept,
I dreamt — marvelous error! —
that it was God I had
here inside my heart.

by Antonio Machado
translated by Robert Bly

6
From Water to Air

When we climb the spiral staircase of the House of Self to the second story, we emerge from the waters of the Solar Plexus into the symbolic air of the Heart and Throat chakras. [See Illustration #10, page 133.] Air symbolizes our ability to think, and thinking enables us to be conscious of self.

The second story of our House of Self was built and decorated in large part by the adults who raised us and educated us. Before the process of awakening began, we occupied this second story in a state of relative unconsciousness. We reflected back the thinking of the primary groups with which we were identified. Or, if our experiences in those groups were painful, we may have reacted against them by developing opposing beliefs and thoughts to represent our rejection of them. Nevertheless, in our reaction we remained identified with them in a negative way.

For example, a friend of mine was raised by parents who were fundamentalist Christians. Their religion was based primarily on emotional fervor. My friend was intellectual by predilection. She had a brilliant mind. She found it offensive that neither her parents nor the pastors of their congregation would entertain any of her questions or address her doubts with other than an admonition to "take it on faith." As a consequence, my friend completely rejected the religion of her parents and became an atheist. She believed that "God" was an emotional crutch and that science could provide answers to her questions that were verifiable and based on reality rather than wishful thinking.

The belief system my friend developed was a reaction to her upbringing, and was a reflection of the attitudes, values, and beliefs of the scientific community. She clung to them as if to a fortification against the onslaught of emotion to which she was exposed whenever she returned home. She was out of the waters of emotion but she had not yet begun to claim the second story of her House of Self as her own.

When the forces are awakened only in the Generative and Solar Plexus Chakras, we use our thinking primarily in conjunction with our feelings and desires. These days I hear young people say, "I'm going to make my first million dollars before I am thirty. Then I will retire and do what I want." They plan for the future, working out strategies for getting what they want, but with little understanding of the larger forces at work in the world around them and of their place within them.

We also use our minds to make sense of our experiences. We attribute motives to other people, rationalize our own behavior, and assess and judge the world around us according to our own values. In these ways we develop a story that describes our lives and who we are, and that private world is what we think is real.

When the yin and yang forces move into the Heart Center, thinking of a new kind is activated. The forces in the Heart Chakra awaken an urge to understand the larger dynamic of things, to see the big picture, to understand others and what makes them function as they do, to know why things are as they are in the world. This is thinking beyond the small environment of our own House of Self. It is like stepping out onto a second-story balcony that completely surrounds the house, giving us a view of the world around us in every direction and far beyond the small neighborhood in which we have been living.

We become aware of how little we know and how little we understand.

What Does Love Have to Do With This New Way of Thinking?

In order to understand the nature of the **Heart Chakra** energies as they awaken, it is helpful to recognize that the **Love-Wisdom Ray** is received by the Heart Chakra and channeled through it. That Ray releases the most beautiful, radiant force in human nature, the love force.

In contrast to what is often called love in the Solar Plexus, which is focused on *getting* what we desire, Heart Center love is motivated by an undeniable *urge to give*. When Heart Chakra energies are stirred and awakened, we tend to pour our energies out to others without wisdom. We are out of balance in the direction of giving, rather than wanting primarily to *possess* a lover or to *receive* love.

Heart Center love gets out of balance when it lacks self-confidence and needs appreciation for what it gives. This need for acknowledgment makes the love conditional. When acknowledgment is not forthcoming, the love can turn to resentment. "Look how much

I've done for you" is a statement we have all heard, and perhaps made, many times. Our nation has fallen into this trap in its foreign policy over and over again.

The outpouring of love from the Heart Chakra needs to be balanced with wisdom and truth. This is the new discipline that must be learned when we are in this phase of the individualizing process.

As the energies are quickened in the Heart Chakra we realize that thinking as we have known it until now cannot always be trusted. We also see that we have little wisdom, even as to what is best for ourselves. **The lesson to be learned in the Heart Center is how to love wisely, in accordance with truth.**

In this phase of our awakening we begin to know that when we are driven by desire, it is not love. When we are driven by need, it is not love. Satisfying desire is only momentary, and meeting needs is not lasting. We begin to see that Heart Center love has a permanence and reality about it that the other motivating forces do not have.

What Are the Lessons We Learn in the Heart Chakra?

When the Heart Chakra energies are quickened, a wide gulf opens between the lower chakras and the upper chakras. The gulf represents our awareness that there is a vast difference between acting as an independent person and acting as one who is contributing to the lives of others. The cleansing of the psyche enters a new phase. We begin to understand that when we are disturbed by what we register from someone else, we cannot blame the other person. We must get the affinity out of our own psyches and then we won't register anything of that quality. We will be able to sustain equanimity no matter what is going on around us.

It is as if we decide, at this point, to recall all the keys to our House of Self. We take keys away from our families and close friends. We clean out their possessions so that we no longer feel they are living in our House of Self. Nothing feeds them. We don't hold any parties at night (in the subconscious). We leave no power on in the lower chakras, no water flows in, and the doors are locked. We learn to lift our forces to the Heart Chakra and above.

We discover, when the Heart Center opens, that *we* control the power. We learn that we can turn the force on and off. We can live in the upper floor of the House of Self if we choose. We do not *have* to be accessible all the time on all levels to all people.

These are hard lessons when we have lived for others all our lives, focused on providing for them, winning their approval, or sacrificing for them. It doesn't feel much like love at first. It feels cold and harsh. We are in dry air now, not warm water. I remember when one of my brothers said to me, during this phase of my awakening, "I liked you a lot better when you were nice." And I remember many times being told by people that they found me unfeeling and cold. Feedback of that kind can be very difficult for those of us who have been people-pleasers for many years!

This is a time of learning to discriminate. We need to be wise and discerning regarding the company we keep. That's why we don't just leave the House of Self unlocked, open to whoever shows up. Instead, we make conscious choices about who and what to let into our consciousness based on the wisdom we are developing through the Heart Chakra.

The tug of war that begins is between motivating forces. Will we continue to be motivated primarily by the urges and desires of the lower centers, or by the motivating forces of the Love Ray? Will we look for the light that pours in through the floor to ceiling doors that open from the second story of our House of Self out onto the heart-centered balcony?

The choice is not a one-time affair, nor is it a matter of "either/or." Just because the ida-pingala forces have moved into the Heart Chakra does not mean they have moved *out* of the lower centers. We will still feel those urges to pursue the activities and persons that will give us personal satisfaction, recognition, and material gain, and serve, create, take action, and express beauty.

Nevertheless, the Love Ray awakens in us sensitivity to the Law of Balance. We recognize that there is a kind of justice at work in the world around us that demands that we recognize the needs of others and work with as much wisdom as we can muster to bring happiness to them as well as to ourselves. We see that in fact we are bound to these others and our destinies are intertwined. When compassion awakens in us, we long to become instruments of good in the world, not for the sake of ourselves alone, but for the sake of all people.

We soon learn, however, that we can also get out of balance if we turn all of our attention to the well-being of others and fail to attend to our own basic needs. In fact, the urge of the Love Ray to pour out energy to others is so powerful that many people give too much. But more about that later.

Our hope lies in learning how to direct the forces at work within us and to have great patience with ourselves while we continue to cleanse our psyches. To come to know the motivating forces intimately, we must be mentally still and try to *feel* our way into them. This is the beginning of the *feel-know,* a new way of coming to know that does not rely on mental processes alone. We begin to recognize the *quality* of the motivating forces at work in us and we weigh them against the urge to love. Are they compatible? Will they serve the higher frequencies into which we are moving?

After Arleen Lorrance had developed the Love Project at a ghetto high school in Brooklyn with life-changing results for the young people who were involved,[1] she was invited to California for a month of training to be a group facilitator. During that time, one of the trainers made a proposal to her. He wanted to spread the Love Project around the nation through a huge publicity campaign that would involve making T-shirts, banners, and posters with the "Love Works" slogan on them. He would promote Arleen as the founder of this movement and see that she got interviewed on all the big television talk shows. He would act as her agent to set up a speaking tour for her, etc.

Arleen looked within and asked herself what would motivate her to do such a thing? The only urge she could find would be the urge to become famous and perhaps to make some money. When she lined that up alongside the motivating force that had brought the Love Project into being, there was no comparison. That urge had not been about her at all. It had been about giving the young people in her high school some

---

1. See *The Love Project,* by Arleen Lorrance, San Diego: LP Publications, 1972.

hope that their lives could amount to something. She had wanted to bring them some joy. She had wanted them to experience unconditional love.

There was no question that the proposal to "take the Love Project nationwide" through a giant publicity campaign would carry a very different frequency and would not be true to the nature of heart-centered love. She turned down the offer.

We also learn to discriminate with regard to people. Even though our information about someone is limited or contradictory, love weighs the truth in its scales. We feel-know the nature of the other, the truth of his or her being.

Recently we were getting estimates from people for some work we wanted done in our home. I had talked with four people to get estimates. One man was very friendly and solicitous and offered to match anyone else's price. He promised fine workmen and top quality products. Although his manner was very pleasing, I did not trust him. I had no reason *not* to trust him, no evidence to substantiate my feeling, and he did give us references to call. Another man was matter-of-fact in his presentation. He said he could not do the work for about two weeks because he was too busy and his price was the highest quote we were given. But I would have hired him without hesitation. The other two fell away for one reason or another.

As my partner and I weighed the data I had gathered, we talked ourselves into hiring the man I didn't trust because he could do the work sooner and his references panned out. When the appointed day came, his workmen did not show up and he did not answer the telephone at his workplace. My heart sank. I had been right in my first impression. We had trouble getting the work completed to our satisfaction. I am still learning to trust the wisdom of the Heart Chakra, which knows the truth in a way that facts and figures can never reveal.

My father was a successful businessman who acted on the wisdom of the Heart Chakra. He once told me that he could tell when someone came through the door of his shop whether he would buy or not and whether he could pay for what he would buy. Dad could not explain how he knew, but he knew, and the truth his Heart Center felt could always be trusted.

This faculty of the feel-know also helps us to find our way to books, groups, and teachers that can help to orient us during our awakening process. By our feel-know we will determine whether or not someone's presentation of the truth is valid, and whether it will foster our growth in consciousness. What other people say by way of recommendation or criticism is of little importance. What our own Heart Chakras tell us is what matters most.

The difficulty with the wisdom of the Heart Center is that we do not come to it by gathering data with the five senses, nor do we come to it by inductive or deductive reasoning. We come to it by direct perception: Heart Chakra seeing, which leads to an immediate knowing. Most of us are reluctant to trust this knowing because it seems to fly in the face of all we have been taught. To develop the feel-know and to trust it enough to act on it takes time and practice.

What Indications Do We Have That the Heart Chakra Is Opening?

Often the first indication that the Heart Chakra is opening is copious weeping. If the force of the Love Ray, that is, the urge to give, has been repressed over the years, and perhaps has turned to resentment, disappointment, or sorrow, that energy must now be released. The release comes in the form of tears, seemingly without provocation.

I remember a man in our Love Family who, following the death of his wife, found himself consumed with grief. Months passed, and the tears continued to flow. He had to quit his job because he couldn't refrain from weeping, even when customers were present or when he was in consultation with his boss. At first he thought he was losing his mind. The loss he felt when his wife died did not seem to account for the degree of grief he was experiencing.

This experience of copious tears continued for several years. Eventually he came to understand that his Heart Chakra had opened and he was being asked to make a larger contribution to the world: a gift of his wisdom. He began to travel from school to school to give talks about peace and how we can learn to live in peace with those who are different from us. Once he began to give from his Heart Center, the tears stopped.

When the Heart Chakra is opening, any grief that has gone unexpressed must be released. Many people say, when the Heart Center tears begin to flow, "I feel I am grieving, but I don't know for whom or for what." They may never remember the specifics, or whether it was in this lifetime or a previous lifetime, but repressed grief must pour out once the frequencies of the Heart

Chakra are quickened.

Others experience an uncontrolled form of grieving for all humanity. When my Heart Chakra was opening, I went through a period of several months when I could not go anywhere where there were crowds of people. I remember the first time I became aware of this new sensitivity. I got out of my car in the parking lot of a large K-Mart store and a huge wave of sorrow washed over me. I burst into tears. The grief was so enormous that I had to get back into my car and, when I was able, drive home. For several days I wept for "humanity." I knew this was not my grief, but the weight of it was enormous.

For months this grief could be triggered by the slightest exposure to "humankind." If I listened to the news on television or read a newspaper, an overwhelming grief would encompass me and I would weep uncontrollably. These tears seemed impersonal. That is, they didn't come in the same way for people I knew and loved. These tears were for strangers, for "all people everywhere" who were suffering or had suffered loss.

Some people experience this same kind of grief for the animal kingdom. Sorrow for the suffering of innocent creatures can be equally intense, and the flow of tears just as plentiful.

It is important to realize that these tears represent a release of pent-up or repressed love-force. The "cure" is to give of oneself, but it is important not to fall into the illusion that by our own efforts we can relieve the suffering of all living creatures. This is why Mother Teresa was such an outstanding example of one who knew how to love with wisdom. She did not try to eradicate poverty. Instead, she set out to love one suffering human being at a time. She poured out her love without expectations that the world would change as a result.

What the Heart Chakra asks of us is to give. It is important not to identify that need to give with any particular person or situation. Sometimes we try to give and find we are rejected. Then we must move on and look for situations where the door is open and our gifts are welcomed. It is not when or how or to whom we give that is important. Rather, it is that we find a channel for this love-force that seeks to pour through us.

I have learned over the years, as a result of some difficult experiences, to wait until I am asked before I give. It is often difficult to wait for someone to provide me with the opportunity to give. But if I jump in without the invitation, I am often seen as interfering. Or, what I give is ignored. When people ask, it is because they are ready to receive. I believe this is one of the keys to wise giving.

Sometimes the opening of the Heart Chakra is accompanied by an apparent physical crisis that will be labeled "heart trouble." Medical doctors may treat the physical condition, but if we do not respond to the urgent inner push to give of ourselves to the world, the physical symptoms will return.

My partner, Arleen Lorrance, was stricken with a viral infection in the lining of her heart when she was only 29 years old. The doctor ordered total bed-rest for six weeks and limited activity for six months. Arleen felt totally debilitated by this physical condition that brought her busy life to a complete halt. However, as she began to regain her strength, her consciousness opened to the possibility of a whole new way of being in the world. Within a year she had given birth to The

Love Project in the ghetto high school where she taught. What had first appeared to be heart trouble was actually an opening of the Heart Chakra. Once Arleen began to pour her unconditional love out into the school environment, her physical health was completely restored.

The subtler symptom of an awakening of the energies of the Heart Chakra is a sensation like millions of butterfly or hummingbird wings fluttering in the chest cavity. If this is not confused with a physical sensation of "something wrong," the wonder of the quickening can be directly experienced.

Why Does the Awakening in the Heart Chakra Bring Such a Radical Change?

The Heart Chakra is the balance point of the psyche. In the Heart Center the yin and yang energies come into perfect balance, enabling us to function through the personality with perfect equanimity. The love that pours out through us is unconditional, universal, and impersonal. In fact, it is the Universal Creative Force that pours through. It is not something *we do*.

The Heart Chakra represents the first awakening of the energies of the Higher Self, Real Self, or Autonomous Field. The description of the Seven Rays helps us to grasp the essential nature of the creative force. It is based on the understanding that the Original One, which in its absolute unity could not know itself, divided into two forces, the yang and the yin, in a process similar to the mitosis of cells. These two forces, often called the positive and negative polarities, or the masculine and feminine, were labeled the Will Ray and the Activity Ray. When they united, a Third Ray came forth as the "child" born of their union. The Third Ray was labeled **Love-Wisdom**.

Thus the symbolism of the Seven Rays suggests that Will, Activity, and Love-Wisdom characterize the essence of the Original One. We come to know those characteristics in ourselves through the Crown, Sacral, and Heart chakras. *In the individualizing process, the Heart Chakra is awakened from within the psyche to prepare the way for the higher frequencies of the spirit.* It is our introduction to the individualized expression *through us* of the Original One.

Though the Heart Chakra pertains to the psyche, it is a foretaste of the Spirit, or Real Self. Through the Heart Center we experience universal energy for the first time, in contrast to the personal energy with which we have been identified until now. This energy is not subject to the whims of preference. It loves, not because of who the other one is or what he or she has done, but rather because it is of the nature of the Heart Force *to love*. The Heart Chakra rays out love like the sun rays out light: whoever and whatever is in its way will experience its unconditional, life-giving force.

It is also the nature of Heart Center love to ask nothing in return. There are no conditions placed on the love before or after it is given. It does not have to be earned or deserved, nor does it have to be returned. For all these reasons it is termed universal, unconditional, and impersonal.

The Love-Wisdom Ray is also called the binding power. It is the energy that flows between the yang and yin, between Will and Activity, holding the two polarities in a union that releases the creative force into the Cosmos. Thus we also experience the power of love, pouring through the Heart Chakra, as a binding power. When a man (yang) and a woman (yin) give birth to a child, the binding force of love holds them together. Nothing ever really breaks that bond. In their personalities the parents and the child may go through many very difficult experiences, but they are still bound in love. Sometimes we stand in awe as we recognize that in spite of the fact that a parent has abused, neglected, or even abandoned a child, the child still loves the parent. Sometimes the love turns to hate, but the bond is just as powerful. There is no way to sever the relationship that brought the child into being.

In Heart Center love we begin to know, then, that we can never be separated from the creative force that brought us into being. We are loved just by virtue of the fact that we have life. It is about this love that Paul wrote, "I am persuaded that neither death nor life, nor angels nor principalities nor powers, nor things present nor things to come, nor height nor depth, nor any other created thing, shall be able to separate us from the love of God" (Romans 8:38-39). The force of love binds us to the One. Coming to know that state of union is the culmination of the individualizing process.

Venus in Libra

This phase of the awakening process is symbolized in esoteric astrology by **Venus in Libra** to help us to grasp the nature of the Heart Center energies as they awaken. **Venus** is, of course, the Goddess of Love, and it is the Love-Wisdom Ray that is received by the Heart Chakra and channeled through it. Venus is also the most beautiful planet in the sky, and thus is a perfect symbol for the most beautiful, radiant force in human nature, the love-force.

The love symbolized by Venus gets out of balance when it lacks self-confidence and needs appreciation for what it gives. That's why Venus is said to be in **Libra** when the heart center opens. Libra, symbolized by the scales, represents the capacity to balance the outpouring of love with wisdom and truth.

The lesson to be learned in the heart center is how to love wisely, in accordance with truth. The key words for Libra are "**I weigh and measure**," and they express the new discipline that must be learned when we are in this phase of the individualizing process, namely, to walk the middle way between the yin and the yang.

Ways to Practice:
    1. **Sit quietly with your feet on the floor and your spine erect. Focus on the center of your chest.** Imagine that there is a huge revolving door there. As you inhale, imagine the air enters the revolving door. As

you exhale, imagine that it exits through your back, between your shoulder blades. Continue to practice this visualization of the process of breathing through the Heart Chakra. It is a way of practicing no attachment to the force of love that moves through the Heart Center.

2. Begin to observe yourself when you experience the motivating force of the Love-Wisdom Ray. Do you feel an urge to give that is so powerful that you can hardly resist it? Do you give indiscriminately (no matter who asks, or what the circumstances are), or do you weigh and measure whether it is wise to give to this person or to this organization or in this situation?

3. Look back over your life. Are there times when you have given too much? How do you know? Was it not the best thing for the one to whom you gave? Or did you regret it afterward because no thank you was forthcoming, or no recognition of any kind? Are there gifts you gave that you still think about, wishing you had not given them? See if you can discover what the real motivating force was behind those gifts. Be totally truthful with yourself.

4. **Are there persons to whom you make yourself available all the time, even when you are asleep or overburdened with other responsibilities?** Can you begin to draw new boundaries, exercising discrimination that decides how much it is *wise* for you to give to this person or these persons?

5. **Can you remember times in your life when you *knew* something to be true (or not true), to be trustworthy or not, without any apparent facts to support your knowing, yet you turned out to be right?** Acknowledge that knowing as a direct perception from the Heart Chakra, an example of the feel-know that opens when the Heart Center energies are activated.

6. **Sit with your feet on the floor and your spine erect. Practice breathing into the Heart Chakra, with your focus of attention on the center of your chest.** Then, as you exhale, let the energy radiate out in all directions, like the concentric circles in water where a pebble has fallen, except spherically. Each time you exhale, let the concentric, spherical waves expand farther until they encompass everyone you know, then your entire city, then your entire state, then your nation, then the entire earth and everyone on it,

and then out into the galaxy and the universe. As you visualize this expansion, know that you are *loving* everyone and everything, universally and unconditionally. Be sure that you experience your own body and personality as enveloped in all that love.

7. Sitting quietly, feet on the ground, spine erect, breathing in and out through the Heart Chakra, ask yourself, "What is wanted of me? How do I fit into the big picture of things?"

8. Do you know that you are loved, absolutely and without reservation, just by virtue of the fact that you are alive?

Notes:

7
Drying Out

In the lunar phase of the process of awakening, a great deal of our time and energy goes into sorting through the contents of the House of Self. Just as the yin and yang energies (the ida and pingala) spiral around the central axis of our energy fields, releasing more and more force through the five chakras that pertain to the psyche, so we keep spiraling through the House of Self, bringing ourselves up to date with our current state of consciousness.

When we speak of chakras opening, we are really referring to an expansion of our self-awareness and of our ability to function consciously in the energy frequencies represented by each chakra. The forces first awaken in the Generative Chakra, but most of us are unaware of that fact until much later. Consequently, we deal with our new awareness as best we can. As the Solar Plexus opens, we may begin to sense a shift in our consciousness, but we might not. Therefore we deal with the consequences of the new energy flowing through the Solar Plexus Chakra without much understanding of what we are doing. Perhaps by the time the Heart Center opens we begin to know that we are awakening, and we may seek books or a teacher who can help us to understand the process.

At that point, we may revisit the Generative and Solar Plexus Chakras in greater self-awareness. As we do so, we will no doubt engage in a second round of cleansing of the earth energies, symbolically represented by the basement. In the light of our new awareness of Heart Chakra frequencies, we may reevaluate what we have inherited from the various groups with which we have been identified. Holding them up to the new standard of unconditional and universal love, we may find that there are many values, beliefs, and habit patterns that are no longer in harmony for us.

For instance, we may have been taught to automatically dismiss whole groups of people as unworthy of our time and attention. Our new intention to open to all people through the Heart Center, receiving them as beautiful and providing them with the opportunity to enrich our lives with their differences, may make that former practice untenable. We sort through all such attitudes and preferences and discard what doesn't serve us. As we grow and change, we keep returning to the basement for this kind of reevaluation.

The same is true of the Solar Plexus. In the initial stages of awareness of feeling responses to various life experiences we may have thought we were undertaking a radical cleansing of the waters of the psyche. Yet in the light of Heart Chakra frequencies we will want to revisit the ground floor of the House of Self. Our sensitivities will have heightened in response to Heart Center awareness, and there may be other experiences from the past that need to be lifted up so that we can experience them again and perhaps discover that we need to forgive others and ourselves for situations that didn't seem serious at the time, but now feel very disharmonious.

I remember a period in my own process when I sat

every morning in meditation and asked for awareness of anyone I had harmed through attitudes, actions, or words. Often what came up were internal processes that had never been outwardly expressed to another. Still, I recognized that in energy I had done harm to the other. I needed to forgive myself for what I had done. Sometimes I wrote to the person to "confess" what I had done and to ask for forgiveness.

I spent several weeks clearing those active actions of harmfulness to others. Then one morning my inner voice said, "What about your godchildren?" I responded in surprise, "What about them?" The response was, "Have you held them actively in your consciousness? Have you contributed to their spiritual development in any way?" Suddenly I realized what was meant by "sins of omission." I had agreed to be godmother to several children and had essentially never given them another thought.

I held each of my godchildren in my consciousness, waiting for inner direction as to what was an appropriate way to relate to each. They have never completely left my consciousness since then.

The awareness of Heart Center frequencies opens our eyes a little wider and we see the first two chakras of the psyche differently. This will be true each time a new center opens. Consequently, we will feel, from time to time, that we are covering old ground with which we thought we were finished. We must be patient with ourselves. The old ground may be familiar, but our sensitivities are different. What was once in harmony may no longer be. That is why we revisit it.

As we work with cleansing the psyche, we seek to have clear waters that serve as a mirror of the Real Self.

Before we entered the lunar phase of the awakening process, the mirror of the psyche was turned outward to the groups with whom we were identified. Thus we were mirroring the values, beliefs, habit patterns, world views, attitudes, etc., of our birth family, our peer groups, the educational system in which we were immersed, as well as our religious communities, fraternal organizations, national and ethnic group psyches.

Once the forces began to awaken us to our potential to function as individuals independent of groups, we began to identify those group influences and to reevaluate them. But the process is a long one, with times of great intensity and other periods of relative ease.

As the yin and yang forces rise into the higher frequency chakras, we begin to turn our mirror upward so that it can reflect the consciousness of the emerging Real Self. As we do that, we want the water to be clear of past memories that cloud the waters, of feelings that cause storms on the surface of the water, and of values that tug on us to return to groups for reassurance, acceptance, affirmation, or approval. We want to be able to still the waters of the psyche to catch a reflection of inner impulses and directives from the Real Self.

Moreover, we may find buried treasures in the waters of the psyche once they are clarified. Sometimes the desires we repress are urges to creativity. When we uncover these unsatisfied urges, we can release the energy and give it expression. We may begin to write poetry, take singing lessons, and begin to paint, sculpt, dance, or play an instrument. We might take up computer design, architecture, or quilting. In effect, a long buried talent may be brought out of the depths of the psyche and be developed in the light of consciousness.

Are There Any Pitfalls in This Cleansing Process?

While in this lunar phase, focused on cleansing the waters of the Solar Plexus, there are three things about which we need to be cautious so as not to get off track in our individualizing process. The heightened energies of the Generative and Solar Plexus Chakras can be the occasion for substituted forms of expression of repressed desires that can be very misleading and deceptive.

For example, if we have repressed desires to be loved, to be intimate with others, to feel important, to have wealth or fame, to be the center of attention, etc., those repressed desires can take the form of religious ecstasies which bring fulfillment in an indirect way. There are many examples of charismatic religious leaders who have built great followings due to their religious fervor, who have fallen into disrepute because of financial and/or sexual indiscretions. We need to monitor our hunger to possess people, things, money, or power masked by the urge to be of service or to express unconditional love. In the individualizing process, it is better to satisfy Generative and Solar Plexus needs and desires directly than surreptitiously because of how easy it is to deceive ourselves and thus get off track in our own development.

To avoid the pitfall of substituted psychic expressions of repressed desires, devotees of the Wisdom in past eras were taught to lift their forces up out of the Generative and Solar Plexus Chakras and into the Heart Center. The story of the Children of Israel passing out of Egyptian bondage represents this kind of passage out of the lower centers. Egypt is a symbol for the Generative Chakra in which the people are slaves to their own

124 THE HOUSE OF SELF

habits and urges. The Red Sea represents the waters of the psyche which sometimes prevent passage into the dry lands of the higher centers. Moses taught the people how to make this crossing on dry land. Moses' parting of the waters of the Red Sea was a metaphor for the potential we have to hold the waters of the psyche in temporary suspension by lifting the energies of the lower chakras, on the breath, into the Heart Center.

Today our unfolding process is occurring so rapidly that it is better to clear the lower chakras by satisfying the urges in those centers, or by attempting to satisfy them until we tire of the pursuit. Here I speak of urges that have not become addictions, but which we might have repressed or ignored while we attended to more urgent motivations.

For example, during this time in our culture certain images are placed before us daily, images of people who are thin, in great physical shape, beautiful or handsome, who make a great deal of money, who drive expensive cars, who are at the top of their career ladders, and who live in large houses. We might take those images in and feel an urge to manifest some of them in our own lives. Then we might put those urges aside in order to raise a family or care for a sick relative. Later, however, the urges will still be there. If we fulfill them, then when we lift the energies into higher frequencies there will be no unfinished business tugging and pulling us back into group identification.

As mentioned on page 91 above, another pitfall of the lunar phase of development is represented by psychic rapport. When the Solar Plexus Chakra has opened to allow more force to flow through, establishing a strong rapport with another can be tantamount to inviting "possession" of our field by another. Such a situation can begin innocently with a feeling of harmony or sympathy. The rapport then grows until we feel everything the other experiences and we no longer know where that one ends and we begin. The feeling of paralysis that results is an indication that we are no longer free agents. We are fused with another and dependent on them for decision-making.

We can also take in physical conditions from someone with whom we form a rapport. I remember years ago the account of a young woman who went to see her boyfriend in the hospital after he was diagnosed with cancer. She was so stricken to see him and to experience his grief over the inoperable cancer that within less than a month she was diagnosed with the same cancer. The same experience happens with healers who do not know the danger of forming a rapport. In their attempt to heal another, they actually take the disease into themselves.

It is vital for all of us to learn to discriminate between the various energy frequencies in which we function. We need to organize our forces by bringing them into consciousness and directing them according to our purpose and objectives. We also need to learn to lift our forces into higher frequencies at will and to know how to close a chakra when we do not want to be unduly influenced by another person.

Below I address the use of the breath for directing energies. Just as we can lift the forces on the breath, we can also pull the energy in and, like closing the lens on a camera, close a chakra. The energy continues to flow internally, but no energies on that frequency can gain access to us from the fields around us nor are we sending energy out through that center.

Finally, there is a danger that as we become familiar with the forces at work in us and through us, we may involuntarily leave our bodies. To *involuntarily* divorce our consciousness from the body is to leave ourselves entirely exposed *in our psyches* to whatever frequencies of influence happen our way with which we are in rapport. It is also possible for other psyches to wander in and take control of our unattended body. Or the body can begin to disintegrate.

It is important to remember that the body serves as a vehicle for our experience and expression, but we are *not* the body. We are the power that is conscious of the body, that identifies with it, and that gives it life. The psyche is also a vehicle for our experience and expression, but we are also *not* the psyche. We are the power that is conscious of the psyche, that identifies with it, and that gives it life. Therefore, as the power to be conscious we learn to take responsibility for the well-being of both body and psyche.

When we go to sleep at night, we withdraw our active consciousness from our bodies. Therefore it is helpful, as we prepare for sleep, to infuse the body with light and peace and with a clear awareness: "This is *my* vehicle." This is analogous to locking our cars when we park them. Such preparation for sleep helps to ensure that the body will not attract any disharmonious entities.

During sleep, most of us remain identified with our psyches rather than dissociating from them. Consequently, our psyches continue to interact and have experiences with other psyches on the astral level and we remember those events as what *"I"* dreamt. In the sleep state, our psyches are highly vulnerable to all the vibrations that surround us and penetrate us, and often those influences linger in our field upon awaking. We cannot shake off what we experience as the "mood" of the dream, or the "presence" of someone who was in our dream.

As we more and more identify with the power to be conscious, we can learn to control the psyche while we sleep by giving it strict directions as to where it is to go and what it is to do, in the same way as we make conscious choices about our associations and experiences while we are awake. It is helpful, for example, to send the psyche to learn something that will advance our state of understanding or unfolding. In that way, it does not just wander about, vulnerable to unpleasant or even harmful influences (which we would experience as nightmares).

It is possible to distance ourselves from our bodies when we are doing breath work or meditating even though that is not our intention. What we want to do is to develop the ability to function consciously *within and through* the body and psyche. However, we can learn how to respond to such an experience.

Usually the urge to withdraw our consciousness from the body is preceded by a feeling of light-headedness and an awareness of a spinning sensation. When we notice either of those two symptoms, we should immediately cease the breathing practice or the meditation, reverse the direction of the spinning, and get up onto our feet, infusing the body with our consciousness. By stomping on the heels forcefully and emitting forceful "huh" sounds in a low pitch, we will feel the psyche come back into alignment with the body.

Sometimes we will begin to feel light-headed or unfocused during the day even though we are not just then doing breathing or meditative practices. When that occurs, it is important to place our attention on our feet, breathing down into the feet and through them into the earth beneath. Stomping on the heels also helps to ground us. It is important to respond to such sensations with calm authority, knowing you are the power of consciousness functioning through these vehicles.

There are many degrees of dissociation from the body. Those who sleep very deeply at night are probably less identified with their bodies than those who sleep lightly or wake often. Persons who are in comas are 100% dissociated from their bodies, unable to respond at all to neural stimuli. If no one else attends to the body of someone who is in a coma, it will disintegrate.

I often think of a story that is told of Ramakrishna, recognized as a saint and master in India in the twentieth century. He withdrew into the mountains, taking residence in a remote cave so that he could meditate without interruption. When he was in a deep meditative state, he was no longer identified with his body or his psyche and his disciples had no way to communicate with him.

One time Ramakrishna had been in deep meditation for about a month, seated in the full lotus position. When his disciples went to check on him, they discovered that maggots had begun to eat away the skin on his legs. They tried to rouse their master to no avail, so they attended to the healing of the wounds in his legs without his conscious participation.

The story illustrates the fact that the body is dependent on our consciousness to infuse it with life and to attend to its needs. Even though Ramakrishna had not totally withdrawn from the body, still he was not infusing it with enough life force to sustain it and the maggots took it for dead.

We may not be advanced enough in meditation to run such a severe risk, but the story makes an important

Drying Out   129

point. It is far better to remain identified with both body and psyche until such time as we have transformed all qualities that do not serve our higher development and have learned how to direct and control our forces in the astral realm.

Toward the end of her life, my mother underwent three surgeries within about two weeks. Each time she was given a general anesthesia. When we are put to sleep with a general anesthesia, we withdraw our consciousness from the body, which is undergoing a procedure that would otherwise be painful for us. After her third surgery my mother had an experience of getting lost on the astral plane and not being able to fully reunite with her physical form.

Even though my mother awoke from the anesthesia and was conscious of her surroundings, she continued to have experiences on the astral plane. She reported her experiences to my siblings, who tried to tell her that these things had not happened or were not happening. But the experiences were so vivid that she remained convinced that they were real, that is, that they had happened in the physical realm. It took her nearly a week to fully reconnect in time and place with her physical body.

When my mother was to go in for a fourth surgery, I told her to promise her body that she would not leave it during the surgery. That she would stay close to it throughout the surgery and be right there when the anesthesia wore off. I told her not to wander off and away from her body. Just before she went into the operating room I reminded her to assure her body that she would stay close. I was, by suggestion, urging her to direct her psyche before going to sleep.

Even though my mother had no understanding of the astral plane or of her capacity for dissociation from the body, when the anesthesia wore off from that surgery she was completely lucid and present in physical time and space.

We all need to understand the natural tendency to withdraw from identification with our bodies as our consciousness expands. Many people talk about "out of the body" experiences as if they were desirable, or evidence of advanced states of consciousness. It is important to realize that letting go of identification with the body and having experiences on the astral plane does not represent advancement.

All of us withdraw active consciousness from our bodies during sleep at night; our dreams represent our memories of some of our experiences on the astral level. However, the experiences we have are usually directly related to our daily lives. That is, we continue to move in the same frequency bands and we remain identified enough with our bodies that it is usually not difficult for us to reorient to physical time and space when we awaken.

To dissociate from the body while awake can be a similar experience, but we are unable to function lucidly on the physical level at the same time. This is why some people who meditate a great deal seem ungrounded and unfocused. Their fascination for the unusual renders them partially ineffectual in the realm of the usual.

When we enter the lunar phase of our unfolding, there is a natural curiosity about functioning on the astral level and having "psychic" experiences. However, until we have undergone a great deal of cleansing and have learned to organize and direct our own forces, it is better not to expose ourselves to random astral frequencies. We will not have changed our level of functioning, but we may well have made it more difficult to take charge of our experiences and expressions. In due time we will be able to choose consciously when to "go out" and when to "come back."

There are persons, of course, who have spontaneously dissociated from their bodies and been transformed by the experience. For the first time they know with certainty, through direct experience, that they are *more* than their bodies and that even if their bodies died, their consciousness would live on. Such experiences have their value and I don't mean to deny that.

Some who are more developed consciously dissociate from their bodies for a purpose. Two friends of mine, for example, choose to "go sit in a tree" when having dental work done rather than to use anesthesia to deaden the pain.

Still, the words of caution given above can serve most people. These words from my teacher Vitvan can help to orient us during the lunar phase of the individualizing process:

> The true orientation of consciousness gives us the ability to function in the objective states of acting, feeling and thinking, **and to be conscious at the same time of the Power with which we act and feel and think.** [Emphasis added.]

Emerging Into Air:
The Power of Conscious Breathing

Of course there is air in earth as well as in water, so when we speak of emerging into the element of air, *we point to developing a faculty of consciousness that is represented by air. That faculty is the ability to think.*

In the evolutionary process, we humans developed the ability to think by abstracting images from the seemingly objective world and holding those images in our psyches. Those picture-images made it possible for us to develop memory, and the labels we gave to the picture-images became the words we used to communicate our memory of our experiences.

The combination of memory with thinking made it possible for us to be self-conscious. That is, we could develop a sense of self because we had a memory of our personal experiences and could talk about them. We became able to reflect on our own activities and to make assessments of them, which provided the basis for conscious choice-making.

The element of air has long been used, in Wisdom Teachings, to represent this development of self-consciousness and the ability to think. In the energetic structure of the individual, the Heart Center is correlated with the element of air. [See Illustration #10.] It is perhaps for that reason that the Greeks thought of the heart as the center of thinking rather than the brain, as is our custom in the Western world today.

When we acknowledge the connection of the element of air with thinking and the ability to be self-conscious, it is easier to appreciate why the breath is associated with the development of consciousness. As we breathe, we literally draw air into our bodies. In the process, we draw in oxygen, which is essential to life. The element of fire is associated with life. It burns at the heart of every atom, and thus in every cell of our bodies. The fire is held in water to insulate it so that it does not consume every configuration of energy, as happens when that fire is released in an atomic explosion.

As we develop, our consciousness will emerge into

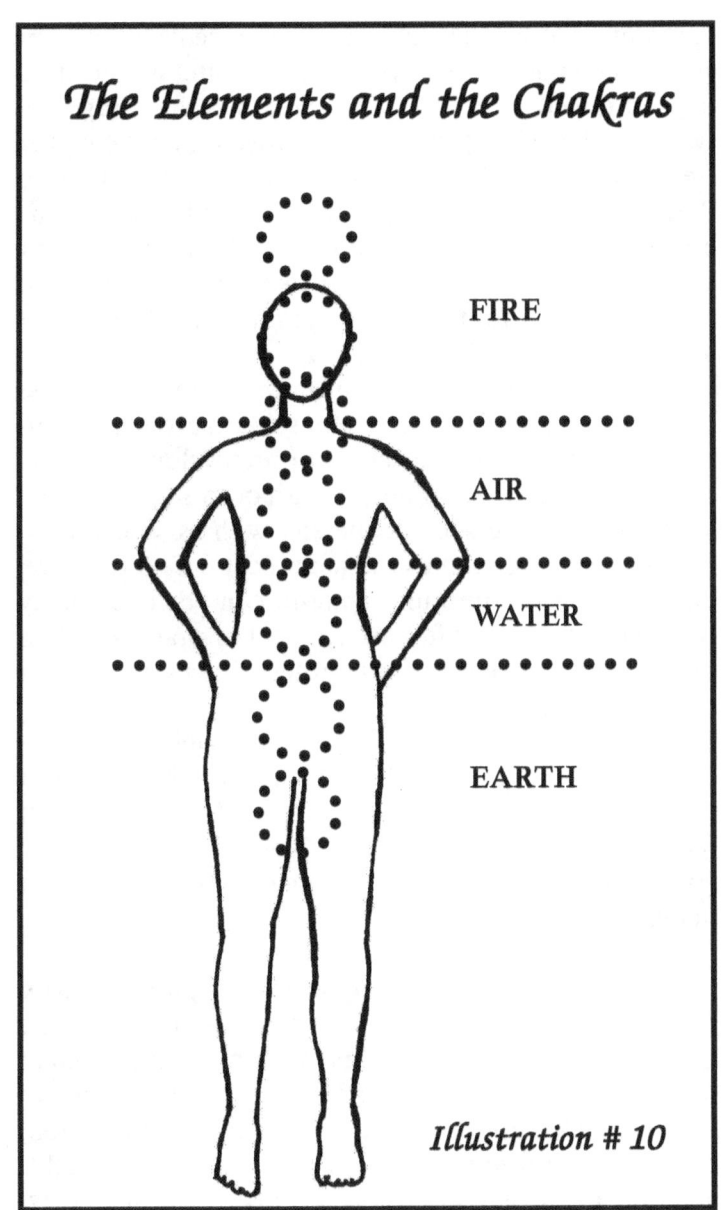

Illustration # 10

the element of fire. The breath helps to mediate this transition, metaphorically drying out the water and feeding oxygen into the fire. Thus the breath is the bridge between the lower frequencies of the psyche and the higher frequency bands. We are able to step consciously onto that bridge by developing our capacity for conscious breathing, which is the key to self-development. It is our access to the individualizing process occurring in us. To cooperate with that process and enhance it, we must learn to master our breathing.

Breathing is the only autonomic function of the body to which we have ready conscious access. No matter how relatively unconscious or undeveloped we are, we can choose to take a deep breath or to stop breathing for a time, and the body cooperates with us. Other autonomic functions, such as the heart beat, blood pressure, digestion, or the immune system, can be consciously controlled, but only after a great deal of practice. Often biofeedback is needed to bring these functions into our conscious awareness.

The breath, however, is readily available to us at every stage of our process of awakening and it is the most powerful tool we have at our disposal. Most of us do not realize that the breath makes it possible for us to take control of both psychic and spiritual forces if we persist in our practice.

In Asia there is a widely used metaphorical story that points out the power of the breath. In the metaphor, the husband (the yang force) is imprisoned in a room at the top of a tower (a symbol for the highest frequencies of the human energy field). His wife (the yin force) comes to visit him under cover of darkness each night, and they carry on conversation. (This represents the cyclic exchange of energy between the two polar forces, occurring in subconsciousness, here symbolized by the night time.)

One night the husband gives the wife the following instructions. "Tomorrow night when you come there will be no moon. Bring along a rope, a heavy packthread, a silk thread, a beetle, and some honey."

The next night, the wife arrived carrying all the items her husband had requested. He then instructed her to tie the silk thread onto the beetle's hind leg, to put a drop of honey on the beetle's antenna, to set the beetle on the tower wall facing upwards, and to play out the thread. The beetle is a symbol for the instincts, the honey represents the promise of self-development, and the thread is the physical breath. By harnessing the instinctual function of the breath and holding in consciousness the promise of self-development, we can reach the highest frequencies of our energy fields with the breath.

In the metaphor, when the beetle reaches the window of the tower room, the husband, or yang force, takes hold of the silk thread and then instructs the wife to tie the packthread onto the silk thread. The packthread symbolizes the force or energy that is flowing through the chakras (the psychic forces), which the yang force is able to control because the breath has lifted it up into the higher frequencies. The husband pulls the packthread up. He then instructs the wife to tie the rope onto the packthread. She does so, and the husband pulls the rope up to the tower window.

The rope represents the power of the kundalini (the spiritual force), which, when lifted up, releases all the power that has been held in check (imprisoned). The husband then ties the rope around a pillar on the tower and shimmies down the rope to reunite with his wife. This represents the descent of the Christos power, sometimes also called the Holy Spirit, which, when united with the kundalini, results in the inner union of the yin and yang. This culminates the individualizing process.

As we move through the description of the various phases of the individualizing process in the course of this book, we describe the process depicted by this metaphor much more thoroughly. The point of telling the story here is to point out that the process begins with harnessing the physical breath. There is no way to stress too much the importance of the tool of conscious breathing.

The key to conscious breathing is the deep, or full, breath. Instead of filling only the upper half of the lungs, we must learn to use our entire lung capacity. To practice, we inhale slowly and deliberately through the nostrils, visualizing that we are filling the lungs with air the way we fill a pitcher with water, namely, from the bottom up. When we reach the end of the breath, we think we have filled the lungs, but usually we can take in more air. So at the end of the breath we then inhale two or three more times, quickly and forcefully. Only then will we exhale, slowly releasing the air through the nostrils.

We never breathe in or out through the mouth. There are several good reasons for this practice. The nasal passages are designed to restrict the influx of air so that it flows in slowly, enabling the lungs to fill completely. As it passes through the nostrils, the air is cleansed by tiny hair follicles and is warmed by the blood vessels that are close to the inner surface of the nostrils. This makes it easier for the lungs to receive and process the air. If we breathe through the mouth, we tend to gulp the air, taking in less than we need to fill the lungs, and the mouth dries out in the process.

To learn this method of deep breathing, we need to practice daily for four to six months before we will master it, unless we have had training in breath control as singers, athletes, actors or orators. In the beginning it is possible that we will experience dizziness from the increase in oxygen rushing to the brain. We can reduce the intensity of our practice if dizziness occurs, but we should not cease it altogether, because with persistence, we will get used to the deep breathing and the dizziness will stop.

As we learn to breathe consciously, we harness air, which is the next frequency band of energies to which we awaken. We can then learn to identify the qualities and characteristics of the energy frequencies in each chakra, to discriminate between them, and to lift the energies from one chakra to another.

To develop these skills, we practice deep breathing through each of the chakras, holding our focus of attention in the area of the body that correlates with those energies. We begin with the Generative Chakra. By slowly breathing in and out through the Generative Chakra, holding our attention focused in it, we become familiar with the characteristics of the energy that vibrates at those frequencies.

After focusing on the Generative Chakra for several weeks, we shift our focus to the Solar Plexus. We become familiar with the characteristics of the energy in that frequency band and begin to learn to discriminate between that energy and the energy that is channeled through the Generative Chakra.

Proceeding thus through the five chakras corresponding to the psyche, we not only come to recognize the different frequency bands of energy, but we also become sensitive to the difference between the frequencies themselves and the content that is loaded onto them. Thus we can quickly identify that someone is approaching us with Solar Plexus energy. What they need or want may not yet be clear to us, since that is the content that will be loaded onto the Solar Plexus frequencies. But before registering a specific, we can already make a choice as to whether to register the content in the Solar Plexus or elsewhere. If we don't want to respond from the Solar Plexus, we can breathe into that chakra, drawing the energy inward and upward, thus effectively closing the Solar Plexus.

The third skill we develop is that of lifting the energies from one chakra to another. As we breathe into a chakra, it is as though the breath is a magnet that draws the energies to it. On the exhale we can imagine lifting the energy up to the chakra that is next highest in frequency. As we inhale again, we do so through the new chakra. Thus we might lift Generative Chakra energies into the Solar Plexus, and then Solar Plexus energies into the Heart Center.

As we develop these skills we will be able direct the forces according to our chosen purpose in any given situation. By lifting the forces from one chakra to another, we help them to begin to resonate with the higher frequencies. Eventually, the entire psyche will be aligned and in harmony so that it is ready to serve as a mirror of and for the true Self.

Ways to Practice:
1. **Sit quietly with your feet on the floor and your spine erect. Resolve to practice the full breath regularly at least once a day for the next six months.** Inhale slowly and deliberately through the nostrils, visualizing that you are filling the lungs with air from the bottom up. At the end of the deep breath, inhale two or three more times, quickly and forcefully, tugging with the diaphragm to expand the lungs so they can hold still more air. Then slowly, deliberately, begin to exhale, releasing the air through the nostrils.

2. **After a week of daily practice with the full breath, continue the practice adding one dimension.** For the first week, hold your attention in the Generative Chakra as you practice the full breath. The area of the lower abdomen, where the genital organs are located, should be the center of your attention, but an entire sphere of energy that extends way beyond the physical body should be included as you visualize the Generative energy spinning slowly, like a pinwheel that radiates energy from the center out into your entire field. Pay close attention to what you experience as you breathe and concentrate on these energies.

3. **In the third week, continue your daily practice of the full breath, shifting your attention now to the Solar Plexus Chakra.** With the area of the navel as the center, visualize a spinning wheel of energy moving out to encompass all the digestive organs and then gradually dispersing energy throughout your entire field. Again, pay close attention to what you experience as you breathe and concentrate. Do not focus on specific feeling states, but on the energy itself.

4. **In the fourth week, continue your daily practice of the full breath, shifting your attention to the Heart Chakra.** With the center of the chest as the center point, visualize a spinning wheel of energy moving out spherically to encompass the lungs and heart and then gradually expanding until it disperses energy throughout your entire energy field. Pay close attention to the quality of this energy. Notice how it differs from the Generative and Solar Plexus energies.

5. **In the fifth week, continue your daily practice of the full breath. Focus first in the Generative Chakra.** Then as you are fully aware of that energy, use the breath, your attention, and your imagination to move the energy up from the Generative Chakra into the Solar Plexus. Feel the quality of the en-

ergy change as you breathe through the Solar Plexus.

6. In the sixth week, continue your daily practice of the full breath. Focus first in the Generative Chakra. Then, as you are fully aware of that energy, use the breath, your attention, and your imagination to lift the energy up from the Generative Chakra into the Solar Plexus Chakra. Feel the quality of the energy change. Then, again using the breath, lift the energy from the Solar Plexus into the Heart Chakra. Again notice the change in the quality of the energy as you breathe through the Heart Chakra.

7. In the seventh week, add one more dimension to your practice of the full breath. As you lift the energy from the Generative to the Solar Plexus Chakra, imagine that you are closing the Generative Chakra so that energy will no longer flow out of or directly into that chakra. You might use the image of a camera shutter that opens and closes, or of a faucet that opens and closes to regulate the flow of water. You will regulate the flow of energy into and out of each chakra by opening it with the full breath and then closing it as you lift the energy into the next highest chakra. This practice will help you to learn to do this in the midst of interactions with other people.

8. Before going to sleep at night, direct your psyche to dip down into its depths, into the metaphorical basement of the House of Self, to find and bring up into the light of consciousness any values, beliefs, habit patterns, world views, attitudes, etc. that are not in harmony with the Love-Wisdom Ray moving through the Heart Chakra. Upon awakening, take a few moments to ask what your psyche has found that needs your attention. As an alternative, this exercise can be done while sitting in quiet meditation and turning your attention within.

9. Turn your attention to the depths of your psyche to see if there are repressed desires buried there that represent unexpressed urges to be creative. What talents have you yet to develop, or what potentials have you not explored? These treasures need to be brought out into the light of consciousness and given your full attention so that what you have always wanted to be or do can now be expressed with enthusiasm.

10. **Observe yourself as you go through your days.** Are there rapports that cause you to give yourself over to others or to let their feelings and thoughts invade your energy field? If so, consciously draw boundaries to separate your field from these others and hold those boundaries firm.

11. **Engage in self-reflection and self-observation to discover:**
a. **What groups no longer serve to advance your awakening?** What values, beliefs, habits, etc. absorbed from those groups do you need to change or release?
b. **What feelings need to be released that you have held on to?** Are there people you need to forgive? Ask forgiveness from? Old wounds that need to be healed so you can move on?
c. **Are there repressed or ignored urges that you need to express and fulfill?**

Notes:

8
Figuring It All Out

To use the metaphor of a House of Self evokes an image of immobility, but it should be apparent by now that the energetic structure of the individual is not in any way static or immobile. It is, in fact, in constant motion. Moreover, when our consciousness of self begins to expand, it is because more power is being released through our energetic structure and our field becomes even *more* active. In this book we are using the House of Self as a metaphor for the fundamental structure of the individual, but we are also describing how our energy field changes as we awaken.

It is important to remind ourselves that in our individual experience the awakening process may not proceed in a sequential order. As we lay out the map in words, labeling each phase as if it were a step on a ladder, the whole process appears to be linear. In fact there are no lines drawn in the energy world and all these chakra energies interpenetrate and commingle throughout our energy fields.

As the chakras are quickened by the creative force rising in the ida-pingala channels (the yin and yang forces spiraling around the sacral-conarial axis as described on page 70 and at the bottom of page 78f), the processes we are describing are set in motion. But they do not start and stop like runners in a relay race. Instead, they move in cyclic rhythms more like the way various instruments of an orchestra play their parts in a symphony. Sometimes we hear the song of the violins and are so captivated by it that for a time we let the other instruments sink into the background of our awareness. But they continue to play nevertheless. Other times the percussion section takes our breath away with its clanging and banging, seeming to drown out the rest. But then the storm subsides and the sweet tones of the wind instruments call us to careful attentiveness lest we miss one note of their delicate contribution.

The opening of the chakras is something like that experience of hearing a symphony. For a time it may seem that nothing is transpiring within us except Heart Center energies urging us to give more love to the world around us. But in the background, the process of awakening continues in the other chakras as well. Thus from time to time we may experience an internal tug of war, as if, for example, we are being pulled by Generative and Solar Plexus energies back into our personal stories. We get caught up in relational dramas from which we thought we had long since freed ourselves. We get our feelings hurt when we thought we were no longer vulnerable to such small affronts. We are suddenly thrown back into old guilt, regrets, and resentments that we have worked with a thousand times in a thousand ways. We cry out in frustration, "What is wrong with me? I thought I had grown beyond this."

It is in those times that we need the disciplines we have been learning, such as how to raise the forces up into the higher frequencies. Toning to clear the channels and lift the forces can be a great help. Chants and mantras that remind us of our true identity strengthen us so that we can break free of the hold these lower frequencies have on us. But deep breathing is our most powerful tool. If we can lift our energies on the breath into the Heart Chakra, we can stand firm there.

Whatever habits we have acquired over the years, it takes at least one-fourth the time we spent cultivating the habits to expurgate them. When this tug of war begins, we can lift those habits into the Heart Center where the forces are balanced and there is no activity, no conflict of any kind. Then if we can hold still mentally and *feel* the power moving through the Heart Chakra, we will observe as these old habits die from lack of attention and exercise. We have to be totally in the here and now, not fighting the habits, but also not feeding them. We focus in the Heart Center on the Presence of the Power. We come to know **I am the Power** and I do not choose to direct this power into those activities.

Not only do we often feel we are being pulled back into situations and experiences that are old and familiar, we can also be thrust forward, seeming to skip several chakras along the way. In my own awakening process in this lifetime, I seemed to go from being asleep (unconscious) to a third eye opening that was so dramatic that it was years before I realized there was more that awaited my awareness. I thought I had experienced the ultimate in one ten-day period.

In the twenty-five years that followed, I "backtracked" to bring into my awareness the other four chakras in my psyche and to free myself from attachments through an intensive cleansing process. I now recognize that it is possible that the forces were quickened in the lower chakras earlier and that it was my conscious awareness that needed to catch up with the process.

As we continue to look at this symbolic map of the

experiences that await us as we are awakening, perhaps we should imagine that we are standing at the center of a circle, and each of these chakra experiences is like a slice of the pie of awakening. We may become conscious of the slices in random order, but when we have digested them all we will be ready to move on to the solar phase of the individualizing process.

What Energy Motivates Us In the Throat Chakra?

In our metaphor of the House of Self we have spoken of the second floor only in passing, for we focused first on the balcony surrounding the second floor, symbolizing the Heart Chakra. Now we turn our attention to the second floor itself. This is the area that houses our thinking function. It was decorated by the adults that raised us, and by all the educators to whom we were exposed. In addition, everything we read or watched on television influenced the way we decorated the second story.

The primary furnishings of this level of the House of Self are picture images of our life experience. Most of them are not original works of art, created directly from our own experiences. Rather, they are reproductions of what we have heard described by others, seen and heard on television, in video games, in movies, in all forms of advertising, and in photographs. The images are stored in both word descriptions and in visual images. Some of them may be audio-images, or aromatic impressions. In other words, these are images stored through impressions registered by the five senses.

While the mirror of the Throat Chakra has been directed outward toward the world in which we are living, we have reproduced within our own energy field the billions of images to which we have been exposed. To those reproductions, we have added a few images of our own, abstracted from life experiences that had a powerful emotional impact on us. Memories of our first experience of falling in love, of times when we felt disappointed or hurt, of significant rites of passage, etc., are stored on the second floor. In fact we not only have picture images lining the walls, we also have large storage cabinets and filing drawers filled with these memories. Scrapbooks were too small to hold our entire life story.

Energetically, the second floor of the House of Self is made up of the Heart and Throat Chakras. It is in these two chakras that we hold our memories, and memories are images held in place by the glue of feelings from the Solar Plexus.

The Throat Chakra, as is implied by the name, is centered in the throat and encompasses the shoulders and the lower part of the face, including the mouth, jaw and ears. Not only do we formulate, or reproduce, picture images in the Throat Chakra, but also we give labels to those images by naming them. So it is in the Throat Chakra that we develop language, and language enables us to both speak and think. The Throat Chakra also makes it possible for us to register the vibrations of thought and speech, both externally and internally. Thus we not only hear others, but we hear our own thoughts and the inner voice of intuition and wisdom. Eventually we also develop the skill of mental telepathy in this chakra.

We utilize the energies of the Throat Chakra to bring order to our internal perception of the world, and through our verbal articulation, to extend that order into the physical realm. When overdone, we can fall into the illusion that through order we can control our world, and we might even attempt to control others by bossing them around.

All of this is a response to the motivating force of the **Ceremonial Ray** that is moving through the Throat Chakra. The Ceremonial Ray motivates us to recognize that all of life is sacred. It awakens in us a reverence for the earth, for plants, for animals, and for all sentient life. We feel an urge to use our mental faculties to understand the universe and our place within it. As our grasp of the big picture grows, we are moved by the Ceremonial Ray to find ways to bring the divine into manifestation through us. We begin to experience a merging of spirit with matter.

The effect of the Ceremonial Ray energies is to awaken an appreciation for order in the Universe. We discover that everything has its right place according to its structure and function. We are then motivated to cooperate with that ordering process by transforming our own lives, making them sacred by putting them in right order. Daily rituals emerge that express our reverence for life in all its manifestations.

Those rituals might seem very mundane, but they are essential to keep us in right relation with our environment: rituals such as the care of our own bodies, the feeding and care of pets we have taken into our charge, the tending of our gardens and yards, washing dishes and clothes, cleaning house, returning phone calls or e-mails as a way of nurturing relationships, preparing meals and enjoying them with family and friends, etc.

The extension of this ordering faculty of the Throat Chakra, motivated by the Ceremonial Ray, is the recognition that all form is quickened and sustained by sound vibrations. When this chakra is opened fully, we will be able to bring things into manifestation just by speaking the word, or by thinking it, since the vibrations of sound stimulate the invisible pattern around which molecules of energy are gathered. Fortunately this creative power is not released fully until all the other chakras are sufficiently developed and the psyche has been cleared so that it reflects only the higher will.

How Can We Recognize The Throat Chakra Opening?

The frequencies of the Throat Chakra are very high. That is, the waves are very short, moving even more rapidly than those "butterfly wings" of the heart center. Not only are there more waves per unit of measured time, but also the crests and troughs of the waves are shallower, making their registry subtler. For this reason, it is very difficult to have anything resembling a sensation with regard to the quickening of the Throat Chakra energies.

However, there are characteristic urges and experiences that can help us to identify this phase of our awakening. The first of these is the urge to make sense of life, of ourselves, and of the world around us. That is, to put things into new mental order.

Generally speaking, when the Throat Chakra is quickened we realize that all the furniture on the second story of the House of Self, namely our beliefs, our world views, our opinions and values, our understanding of self, of others, and of life in general, were all inherited. Suddenly they feel old-fashioned to us. We want to clear them all out and start over, making decisions about how we will redecorate so that the second story of the House of Self expresses our uniqueness.

We determine to figure everything out. We begin to analyze everything, including everyone we know. We long to put everything in conceptual order, to find a place for everything, to make it all fit.

When the Throat Chakra opens, therefore, we tend to reexamine all our old ways of thinking and believing. Often we are tempted to throw out the old and start over to build a world view, a way of understanding life. However, we want our perception of things to be true, so we search for guidance from authority figures who can help us to grasp the true nature of things.

I remember thinking, when my Throat Chakra opened, that nothing I had ever been taught or had ever believed was relevant in any way. I didn't even want to use the word "God" in developing a new way to talk about what I was coming to know. The word "God" was weighted down with old concepts and images that no longer fit my experience of life. I felt there must be a way to talk about the nature of reality that was not faith-based, as the religion of my upbringing had been. Eventually I found my way to the philosophy of yoga. It appealed to me because it was described as a science, not a religion.

The urge to bring new mental order to our lives is an expression of the influence of the Ceremonial Ray, which motivates us to see everything as an essential part of the whole. It causes us to long to see how everything fits together according to a natural order. We seek out individuals who seem to perceive that order and invite them to provide us with words and images that will enable us to think about and understand the world the way it is in reality, that is, as an energy system.

Is This Just a Process of Thinking Things Through?

Though we are using our thought processes to reconstitute our mental grasp of the nature of reality, another faculty opens during this phase that changes the nature of our reasoning process. The yin and yang forces release in us a new faculty that can be called *perceptive cognition*. This is *immediacy of knowing by frequency registration.*

Prior to the quickening of the Throat Chakra energies, our thought processes were based on sensory data. We could engage in either inductive or deductive reasoning, but both were based on our experience of the world through our five senses. After the quickening by the yin-yang forces, we begin to register the energy world itself, even if we are not yet conscious that we are doing so.

The faculty of perceptive cognition enables us to know some things without knowing how we know. It represents the beginning of the development of what some call the Noetic Mind, or the Higher Mind, which knows through direct perception. In this early stage, we begin to register frequency, but without clear understanding of the process.

Perceptive cognition is not unlike the feel/know of the Heart Chakra. Both are frequency registration. The difference between them may be difficult to discern at first. However, the Heart Chakra feel/know is more like feeling than thinking. It has no logic to it, but it is powerful in its knowing. Perceptive cognition, on the other hand, is closer to thinking than to feeling. It is related to direct observation and we can more easily explain what we know because we can tie it together with facts from our memory. Nevertheless, we come to the knowing directly, not through a reasoning process.

Thus during this phase of the awakening process we develop certain strong convictions about the way things are, based on our own frequency registration. However, we are likely to use the words of authority figures to talk about what we know rather than to stand in our own authority. We quote other people, refer people to books we have read, and delight in hearing lectures or attending seminars where respected scholars or authorities are expounding upon the very subjects that are of most interest to us.

This may help to explain much of what is known as "channeling." Individuals who channel register the knowing directly but are not ready to stand alone in saying "I" know this. Consequently, they attribute the knowing to entities in the astral world, asserting that the entities are using them to make their views known.

It might be simpler, and more descriptive of this phase of the awakening process, to say: "This is what I know. I don't know *how* I know it, but I do know it."

I began to have this experience strongly not long after my awakening to cosmic consciousness. One morning in my meditation I received an inner directive to start teaching a class on the chakras. I argued with the directive, saying, "I can't do that. I don't know anything about the chakras." That was my objective state of consciousness speaking. Since I had not read about the chakras, nor been taught about them, how could I possibly know anything about them?

My inner voice said, "You will be given what you need to know."

I viewed the whole idea as ridiculous and did not

intend to offer a class. A few days later I attended a cocktail party at the home of some good friends. I had just walked in when a woman came up to me and introduced herself as the next-door neighbor. She asked, "When are you going to start your class?" I said, "What class?" She looked startled. "Aren't you going to offer a class? I thought you were." Now it was I who was startled. I responded with humility. "Well, yes. Why don't we start next Tuesday evening at my house?"

I passed the word that we would have a class called "The Peacemakers," and at the first meeting twelve people showed up. On the morning of the announced beginning, I sat in meditation and asked, "What do I need to know?" I registered knowing about each of the chakras in turn, for five weeks. Part of my consciousness felt embarrassed to be teaching this information, because I did not know how I knew what I knew. But teaching it felt as natural as if I had always known about the chakras and how to direct energy through them.

I had a similar experience some years later when I asked in meditation, "What is wanted of me next?" I received an inner directive to write the esoteric meaning of the life of Jesus. I refused, saying I didn't know enough to write such a book. After about three months my hands had swollen up and gotten so stiff I could hardly use them anymore. I sat in meditation one morning and asked what was wrong with my hands. The answer came immediately: "The energy for the writing of the book on Jesus is gathering there because you refuse to write." So I agreed. I would begin the next morning.

I sat in meditation with a pen and paper in hand. What I registered as knowing about the inner meaning of Jesus' life came so quickly and simply that the little book *Cosmic Unfoldment* was written in less than two weeks' time. What I wrote seemed true to me, and helped me to express the new understanding of Jesus' life that I was coming to. But I had no explanation for how I knew what I wrote. It truly felt "channeled."

These are two examples of the faculty of perceptive cognition, or knowing by direct frequency registration. It is like picking up a radio or telegraph transmission. The information is there for the having. All we have to do is acknowledge it and be willing to pass it along.

Is the Information We Receive Personal or Universal?

Usually what we register in this way is not just for our own benefit, but also serves the larger good. These are not "personal" messages; they are impersonal truths waiting to be shared with others. Just as the force of love in the Heart Center is characterized solely by the need to give, so the knowing that registers in the Throat Chakra has only one need, and that is to be utilized in service to others.

For this reason, many who experience Throat Chakra awakenings become almost fanatical in their desire to share what they know. They feel an urgency born of a sense that this information is not for them alone: others need to know it and to benefit from it. If such a one finds a receptive group with whom to share, the knowledge can be used as a fulcrum for the joint activities of a group dedicated to the betterment of humankind in one form or another. Those individuals who are not able to find an outlet for their knowing can become frustrated and shut down. Their process of awakening is then blocked.

An example of passing along a message received

and in the process benefiting thousands of others is one familiar to all who have worked under the auspices of Teleos Institute. Arleen Lorrance received by perceptive cognition the six **Love Principles** back in 1970. She set out immediately to share what she had seen, what she knew. First she shared the principles while working with a small group of students and teachers in the ghetto high school where she taught. Later she traveled around California sharing the story of the transformation of that high school through the activation of the Love Principles. Next, she wrote a book called *The Love Project*.[1] Over the course of the next thirty (and more) years, she taught the principles through workshops and practice sessions, in speeches at conferences, through other books written, and through the circulation of small wallet-sized cards on which the principles are recorded.

As a result, thousands of people have been exposed to the principles and have been able to open their own Heart Chakras by actively applying the six Love Principles in their personal life circumstances. Meanwhile, the message of those principles continued to be transmitted by frequency-registration so that by now the principles are widely known and used in a multitude of contexts. Arleen was one who passed on the message, but she was by no means the only one. It was time for the larger group to have knowledge of how to open the Heart Center and live in unconditional love, and the Love Principles made a major contribution to that process.

It is important for all of us to recognize that what we have received by frequency-registration, we must pass along. To be able to communicate what we have regis-

---

1. San Diego: LP Publications, 1972.

tered in frequency requires a concentrated process of holding the frequency while searching for words, expressions, images, or metaphors that can carry the frequency. This requires careful inward listening and precise selection of the best means of communicating what we have received. In other words, this is very conscious communication in which the inner experience and the outer expression must match as closely as possible.

If we do not find an outlet through ordinary forms of communication (writing, speaking, teaching, preaching), we can work in energy to pass the message along, like being a radio relay station. In that way we not only share guidance and useful information so that any who are able to register it can do so, but we also strengthen and accelerate all creative endeavors born of such frequency registration. There are many persons who receive such messages who work exclusively on frequency levels to pass along what they have received.

If we repress the forces being released in the Throat Chakra, or do not find a way to release them, we may experience a sense of fullness or throbbing in the throat, excess tension in the neck, voice interference such as raspiness, and irregularities in pitch similar to voice changes at puberty. Such symptoms are reminders that the urge to share what we register in frequency demands our response.

We can contribute to the expansion of group consciousness in a large variety of ways. What is important at this phase of our development is that we not impede the release of information and ideas by repressing our own urge to share what we know, whether or not we know how we know it.

Mercury in Virgo

In the roadmap provided by esoteric astrology, **Mercury in Virgo** symbolizes the quickening of the Throat Chakra. The key words for the sign of **Virgo** are "**I analyze.**" We determine to figure everything out. Virgo represents a discriminating nature that likes to put things in order, to find a place for everything, to make it all fit. It also symbolizes respect for authority.

When the Throat Chakra opens, therefore, we tend to reexamine all our old ways of thinking and believing. Often we are tempted to throw out the old and start over to build a new world view, a way of understanding life. However, we want our perception of things to be true, so we search for guidance from authority figures who can help us to grasp the true nature of things.

This is knowing through frequency response and is symbolized by **Mercury**, who was a messenger of the gods. He is represented with wings on his heels because he traveled with such swiftness. For this reason he was associated with this new faculty of the immediacy of knowing by frequency registration.

Thus when we are in the phase represented by Mercury in Virgo, we develop certain strong convictions about the way things are, based on our own frequency registration, but we are likely to use the words of experts to talk about what we know rather than to stand in our own authority

Usually what we register in this way is not just for our own benefit, but also serves the larger good. The symbolism of Mercury as a messenger of the gods suggests that what we register is like receiving messages from the greater ones who have preceded us in the awakening process. These are not "personal" messages; they are impersonal truths waiting to be shared with others.

Ways to Practice:
1. **As you continue to practice your full breath, add the Throat Chakra to the mix.** Practice breathing through the Throat Chakra by focusing your attention in the area of the voice box and imagining a vortex of energy that whirls like a pinwheel, circulating energy that encompasses your throat, shoulders, mouth, jaw and ears, and then expands out through your entire energy field. Become acquainted with the qualities of this energy so that you recognize when you are functioning through it.

2. **Continue to practice the full breath, lifting energy from the Generative to the Solar Plexus to the Heart and then into the Throat Chakra.** Also, practice opening and closing the Throat Chakra. Gain control over these energies so that when you want to express yourself in words, or to give order to your world through thought, you can do so effectively by breathing through this chakra and energizing the activities motivated by the Ceremonial Ray.

3. **Practice using your voice to release power through your field.** Use Toning, a method of releasing sound to energize your whole field. [See *Toning*, by Laurel Keyes, Marina del Rey, CA: DeVorss & Co., 1990, and *Healing Sounds: The Power of Harmonics*, by Jonathan Goldman, Rockport, MA: Element Books, 1995.]

4. **Practice chanting as a way to create your energetic reality consciously.** Chants can reinforce your sense of self as an individualized expression of the Original One. Utilize chants such as "I am the power to be conscious, I am the power to be free; I am the power to be conscious; I am the power to be me;" "The I am which is my true Self is the power with which I am conscious of my

world;" and "Freedom I am, Focus I am, I am the consciousness within my soul. I have no beginning and I have no end. All is I Am."

5. Take time to find words that express what you know. Write them, speak them, and sing them with power.

6. If you uncover old beliefs, ideas, or concepts that no longer serve you, breathe them out onto the balcony of the House of Self and hold them there, aware that they are held in the Presence of Power. Do not give them any more attention than is needed to keep them held in the Heart Center. Watch as they begin to die from lack of attention and exercise.

Notes:

"We live in the cosmos not as exiles yearning for the absolute but as alchemists and artists, teasing the shape of the divine emerging out of the eternal and into the now."

– *Cynthia Bourgeault*

"Creation itself belongs to the divine. Our role is more a creative midwifery that has to do with intuiting the new patterns as they arise in the imaginal and helping birth them into form."

– *Cynthia Bourgeault*

9
Reflecting the Light

The ceilings of our metaphorical House of Self can be seen as a series of mirrors. Looking up, we see a reflection of our own state of consciousness. Standing in the basement looking up at the floorboards of the first floor, we see that we are a product of our genetic heritage and of our upbringing. We recognize that we belong to certain groups and that is how we know who we are.

When we climb up onto the first floor of the House of Self, we look up and see reflected back that our feelings are the result of the experiences we have had. We could not help feeling rejected if we were rejected or feeling loved if we were loved. Outer circumstances and other people make us feel what we feel.

Standing on the second floor of the House of Self we look up and see that we are defined in large part by what we think. Our beliefs, values, and opinions are a clear expression of who we are. If people don't agree with us, we know they don't like us or approve of us and we feel rejected by them. If we can't convince them to change their minds, we often turn away from them, preferring to keep company with people of like mind.

By stepping out onto the balcony of the Heart Chakra we are able to gain a much wider perspective, but then we cannot see ourselves at all when we look up, because there is no mirror to reflect back to us. On the balcony we look into the metaphorical sky and see a universal view of humankind. The broader perspective is important, but it does not change our understanding of who we are.

When we finally climb the narrow spiral staircase into the attic of the House of Self, as we do when we enter the Third Eye Chakra, we make a startling discovery. We can look down through the floors of the House of Self and begin to see with clarity who we really are and how we function in reality. This is because instead of a mirror in the attic ceiling there is a skylight which allows light to shine through from the Crown Chakra. In that light the whole House of Self is made translucent and we can see things clearly, both in our own energy fields and in the fields around us.

The faculty of consciousness that is awakened in this phase is *intuitive awareness*. We are not yet functioning by direct perception, but we are learning to see a much clearer reflection of reality. We begin to have a feeling for what it will be like to function directly in the Noetic Mind, that is, in conscious Knowing.

The final stage of the lunar phase of the individualizing process is launched when the yin and yang forces reach the Third Eye Center. The psyche still functions by reflection, but a very important shift in orientation occurs when we enter this phase of the awakening.

How Can We Recognize the Energy of The Third Eye Chakra?

The center of the vortex of energy called the **Third Eye Chakra** is associated with a point between and just above the eyebrows at the center of the forehead. Internally, it is coupled with the pineal gland. It might better be labeled the "three eyes" center, for it relates to three different levels or ways of seeing.

The first eye is the one with which we are all acquainted. It is the kind of seeing that depends upon sensory data. We register light rays reflected off of objects in the world around us and we form images in our consciousness that we then identify with the object. In fact, of course, we are only discerning the peripheral outlines of any given "thing," but the image we form seems real to us. This we call "physical" seeing.

When we are functioning only through the first level of seeing, our perceptions feed directly to the Throat Chakra where they are held as images with their "names," the words we associate with the images. Thus physical seeing functions in the element of air.

The second eye, or level of seeing, might be called the psychic eye. With it we are able to perceive what is not available to our physical senses, but which nevertheless appears to have form. This form is in the astral realm. It can move through objects in the physical world. With our psychic eye, we can perceive these diaphanous forms as well as the color of the astral energies that surround physical forms, often called their auras, and the color of beings in the psychic realm.

Most of us have had a vicarious sample of the nature of psychic seeing (in black and white, and mostly gray) when we have seen the images of our bodies on x-ray films or in digital images during or after various kinds of scans. Lines are not distinct between one organ and another and what we are viewing is somewhat unclear, yet if we are looking at an infant in a mother's womb, for instance, we can discern that it is an infant and we can identify the form and shape of the fetus.

The third level of seeing for which the entire chakra is named makes it possible for us to see the energy world itself. In this realm there are no forms as we know them on the physical level. There are, rather, streams of force and particles of energy. It is difficult to describe what it is like to perceive energy directly. It can be something like seeing the heat waves that rise off of hot asphalt in the summer. It can also be similar to what some people describe as "seeing air," as if small, transparent bubbles compose the air around us. What I know through my own experience is that once you have seen the energy world as it is in reality, you will never again view the physical or psychic realms as "real" in any ultimate sense. You will know that truth is to be found in the energy world.

Seeing of this Third Eye kind must be almost immediately transmuted into metaphor or symbolism or we will miss the experience we have just had. When I first saw myself as an integral part of the Whole, for example, I said, "It is as if everyone and everything is a grain of sand in a large cosmic beach. I am one grain of sand, no more and no less than anyone else. In that sense I am insignificant, and yet if I didn't exist, the cosmos would not be what it is." I had "seen" this truth, but there was no way to describe what I had seen except through metaphor. I have heard others make similar references to grains of sand to express their seeing of the energy world. The truth I came to know through that perception was that I am of ultimate worth and nothing can take that away from me. And, I am an integral part of the Whole. I can never be separated from it and I am never alone.

Here's another example. I have twice perceived the energetic streams that flow from a person's back. I would describe the energy as coming from between the shoulder blades. The pattern of the streams of force, if I had drawn it, would have resembled large wings. These experiences helped me to understand why artists have drawn angels with wings. It is possible that these streams of energy develop when a person's Heart Chakra opens. I do not know. But I do know that the suggestion of energetic "wings" was very strong indeed, and that I knew these two people were highly developed on energetic levels when I saw those streams of force.

The energies of the **Science Ray** pour through the Third Eye Chakra, motivating us to seek to *know by direct experience.* An urge awakens in us not just to have information, but also to know *the truth.* It leads to the searching, analysis and development of ideas, which in the end produce nothing less than profound insight, understanding, and eventually wisdom.

When the urge to know moves us, we are willing to read and listen and consider what others have discovered through their life and experience, but we will want to test everything out for ourselves. Only when we have proven things through our own experience will we be satisfied. Patience develops, because we sense that only over the long haul will we find truth. We use a combination of patient observation, experimentation, painstaking research, and analysis to come to know through this Chakra. *Intuitive awareness* develops over time, and we *see and know* simultaneously.

How Will We Know When the Forces Reach The Third Eye Chakra?

The frequencies of the Third Eye Chakra are even subtler than those of the Throat Chakra, so we are unlikely to have any physical sensations of the awakening of these energies. There may, however, be several stages or phases of this awakening of which we can easily be aware.

An initial phase may come when we develop a practice of meditation. Meditation is an exercise in concentration. By holding our thoughts focused on a question, an external object, a symbol, or a person, we align ourselves in frequency with the object of our concentration. In time we register the answer to the question, the essence of the object, the truths represented by the symbol, or the qualities of being that characterize the person.

As we practice meditation we soon become aware that we are living in a sea of thoughts, and that those thoughts are constantly influencing us even when we are not aware that they are. As we become more conscious of this sea of thoughts, we learn to use our intuition to identify the quality of the thoughts passing through and the frequencies on which they are carried. Then we can learn to fine-tune our registry so that we bring in thoughts that are in harmony with the reality we want to create and live in rather than registering any or all thoughts indiscriminately.

We also begin to recognize that every thought we think adds to the color and shape of the energies flowing around others. Our thoughts help to create the group realities we all live in. We learn to guide and direct our own thoughts so that we influence others in ways we choose consciously.

We also learn that we can communicate with others at a distance by tuning in to shared frequency bands. We receive thoughts (messages) sent out by others and, with practice, we also learn to send out thoughts or impressions we want others to receive.

Another phase of the quickening of the third eye center may be our discovery of the constant flow of archetypal patterns and abstract ideas moving through our awareness. For example, we may never have even thought about the Great Mother before. Suddenly we find that even the most ordinary things, such as plants in our garden, turn our attention to the Great Mother. We find ourselves thinking, "I don't even know what the Great Mother is." So off we go to research the Great Mother, to learn as much as we can *about* her. But that doesn't quench our thirst for knowledge of the Great Mother. Somehow we must come to know her directly. We open our consciousness to this possibility and let ourselves be guided to experiences.

I remember keenly an experience I had following my first trip to India and Nepal. There I had been introduced to the Goddess Kali. I had not heard of her before that trip, and I absorbed information about her throughout the trip, including hearing about the severe test small girls go through in Nepal to become the "Living Goddess," a representation of Kali in the flesh. These little girls had to spend a night in a dark area surrounded by the heads of bulls that had been sacrificed to Kali. If they could live through the night, surrounded by the sight and smell of the blood, without becoming frightened, they could be considered for the privilege of being a living representative of Kali.

I had seen pictures of Kali, her long fingernails

dripping with blood, a necklace of skulls around her neck, and I knew her to be the Goddess of destruction and death. But all of this was knowledge "about" her. She was not yet in my own direct realm of knowing.

Then one day, during a Rolfing[1] session, I was swallowed by Kali. This was an internal experience that went beyond visualization. I had not been thinking about Kali nor visualizing anything as the Rolfing practitioner worked on my back. But suddenly I looked down into Kali's blazing eyes. Her mouth was wide open, like an enormous snake. She began to swallow me whole, from the feet up. I watched it happen, and then I was inside her. The sense of peace and security was astonishing. I remained in Kali's belly for several days before I emerged.

During that entire time I kept feeling how wonderful it was to be swallowed whole. It was clear to me that Kali wanted *all* of me, not just the socially adapted parts of me, the "good" parts of me. Over and over again I thought, "It is wonderful to have a mother who is not 'nice.'" When I emerged from Kali, I felt whole. Any sense of the good and bad dichotomy within me had been transformed into unity. In addition, I felt totally accepted and loved just as I was. Nothing would ever be able to take that feeling away from me.

This was an "experience" of an archetype: coming to know it through direct experience. Other archetypal images and patterns that might come into our awareness are the Christ Child, Christ Consciousness, the Grand Architect of the Universe, the Destroyer, the nature of Good and Evil, the Collective (or Universal) Conscious-

---

1. A method of deep-tissue massage called Structural Integration, developed by Dr. Ida P. Rolf in the mid-twentieth century.

ness, Elementals, the Devil, Death, Rebirth (or Reincarnation), etc. These are only a few examples. We will discover many others, and they will haunt us until we come to know them through our own experience.

Many different abstract ideas might come into our consciousness. Not long ago a friend said, "I've been thinking about human beings. Just what does it mean to be human, anyway?" She was clearly not looking for a one sentence answer on the mental level. Something had awakened in her in the Third Eye Center that was demanding to be known at a higher frequency. Something that would encompass all she already knew and much, much more.

Abstract ideas in the Third Eye Chakra stretch the limits of our mental perception and then press us beyond into the vast unknown. We pursue because **if it came to us to wonder, then it** *can be known.*

We have many examples of this among our scientists. For example, for many years now physicists have been searching for "a theory of everything." This is a very abstract idea, yet one that will eventually bear fruit, because if we have the question, the answer is waiting for us and we will find it.

Another awareness that begins to dawn in the Third Eye Center is that mental images are the first step in bringing invisible patterns into form. Thoughts based on those images are the second step as we work with abstract ideas, or archetypal patterns, to bring them closer into manifestation. This is **the inherent creativity of the Mind**.

By turning the mirror of the psyche upwards to the Light, we can become co-creators in the ongoing process of bringing new realities into being. All inventors utilize this Third Eye faculty. They get an idea, which is based on an archetype as all "new" ideas are. Let's say the idea is of a portable chair to be used on field trips. Once the inventor has the idea, he then must think through how to make it. Only then will he be ready to gather the materials and give it a try.

We've all heard stories about Thomas Edison who said, "Genius is one percent inspiration and ninety-nine percent perspiration." When he registered an abstract idea, he knew it was possible to bring it into manifestation. He had dozens of young people working with him in his laboratory for an average of 55 hours a week. When they kept failing to make something work, he would encourage them to keep trying. He once said, "Results? I have gotten lots of results. If I find 10,000 ways something won't work, I haven't failed. I am not discouraged." On another occasion he said, "I would construct and work along various lines until I found them untenable. When one theory was discarded, I developed another at once. I realized very early that this was the only possible way for me to work out all the problems." Even with dozens of workers helping him, it took nearly ten years to invent the alkaline storage battery and longer than that to find an electric light bulb that was practical and long-lasting. Harnessing the physical energies of the Sacral and Generative Chakras to give an abstract idea form can be a long and arduous process.

At this stage we also discover the power of symbols as mediators between archetypal patterns and abstract ideas, which are only vibratory patterns and have no form, and the realm of mental images. Symbols, which we might describe as abstract or archetypal images, act as magnets to hold the invisible in our consciousness until we can grasp it in mental images and then in thoughts. One time I was given instruction in my sleep about healing. When I woke up, I could not remember the instruction, but I knew that as the "teacher" had talked he had shown me an equal-armed cross and had pointed to the center of it. "That is the secret of healing," he had said.

For years I meditated on the equal-armed cross as a symbol. I was able to manifest what I had learned some years later. I had a rash under my breasts which had been bothering me for weeks. I had tried many treatments and nothing made it go away. One day I was drying after a shower and I looked at the rash. It looked red and angry and it itched. In that moment my desire to be rid of the rash aligned with my will and I spoke out loud with great authority, saying, "That's it! Finished." The rash disappeared almost instantaneously. I could feel that my desire and will aligned on the vertical axis of the "cross." The rash was on the horizontal axis. When the two intersected, the healing was immediate.

Symbols provide us with access to abstract ideas and help us to connect with the knowing of how to bring the abstract into tangible form. They are like doorways to the creation of new realities.

It should be said that the images we touch in the Third Eye Chakra are not necessarily visual. They also come as sounds, shapes, spatial locations, and even mathematical formulas. The four archetypal representations of reality recognized by all sciences and cultures are numbers, music, geometry, and cosmology. With our intuition we can tap into any of these universal languages and capture the reflection as images in our psyches.

An example of a nonvisual registry of something abstract is one of the most common indications of a third eye opening. It is the registry of the vibrations of the whirling molecules of energy at the most fundamental level of cosmos. Many refer to this as hearing the cosmic OM, said to be the first act of creation that set the energy in motion out of which everything extant was configurated. Others refer to hearing the sound currents, or the music of the spheres.

When I first heard these sounds I called them the sound of silence, since I heard them only when I was able to still all my thoughts and feelings and listen beneath and behind environmental sounds. For some these sounds are like a low rumble, or a roar. For others the sounds are high-frequency ringing and singing. I suspect the sounds actually encompass the entire range of possible frequencies. The Hermetic principle "everything is vibration" becomes a vibrant knowing through experience once you have actually *heard* the vibrations.

Finally, as the Third Eye Center quickens, we begin to perceive different levels of reality. We may begin to sense the presence of entities who are functioning on the astral plane but not on the physical. We may actually *see* them, or we may just know that they are there though we cannot see them. We may also hear them and even be able to converse with them.

We may also find that we are no longer bound by the time constraints that seem to govern our physical reality. We may begin to know what is going to happen before it happens. Or we might see past incarnations, including our own. When past, present, and future all seem available to us, this is an indication of a Third Eye Chakra awakening.

Sometimes, if our identification with sensory perception is too great, the quickening of Third Eye Chakra energies may be experienced as congestion in the forehead, as headaches, a throbbing, buzzing, or pounding in the head, ringing in the ears, excessive warmth, heat or burning sensations in the head, light-headedness, or dizziness.

If any of these symptoms are indications of the ida-pingala currents having converged in the Third Eye Center rather than some physical ailment, they will be relieved by using the breath to lift the energies up through the Crown Chakra where they can be released, or by directing the energy on the out-breath down to the Sacral Chakra and out through the feet.

What Does Intuitive Perception Reveal to Us?

When the Third Eye Chakra is fully awakened, it will be as if all the secrets of the universe are revealed, even though what we see, and thus come to know, is only a reflection of the real. If it is a clear reflection the light will be bright enough to truly illumine, not only our seeing, but also our understanding. I remember the thrill, during the weeks and months following my Third Eye Center awakening, of being able to pick up any piece of inspired writing and enter directly into the frequency in which it was written. As I read, I perceived directly the meaning the author had intended to convey without needing to activate any thoughts. I was in an immediacy of perception. What a gift!

When such *intuitive awareness* is awakened, there are several things we see and know. First, we see that **there is only One.** This is a major realization that completely obliterates the consciousness in which we have been living, namely, that our world is made up of multitudes of separate "things:" millions of people, animals, insects, reptiles, and fish; an astonishing variety of plants, minerals, gemstones, rocks, etc. We have seen all of this as a world made up of differences that separate and distinguish one thing from another.

Suddenly, in the bright light of the clear reflection of Crown Chakra energies, we see that **there is really only One.** Everything is a Unity. All formerly separate things are actually part of one whole. This astonishing realization leads to a second perception.

There is no death. When we become aware that there is only One, we can see that we are essential parts of the Whole. There is no way the One can be what it is if any part of it ceases to be. Therefore, there can be nothing like what we think of as death, namely, the cessation of existence. If any one of us were to cease to be, the One would no longer be what It Is. What a revelation!

Third, we see that **everything is perfect just as it is.** This we can see and recognize because the One is whole and complete. It is not in a state of becoming. It already Is. Therefore, nothing is lacking. Nothing is needed. Everything just is.

Fourth, we see that **each of us is an expression of the One.** If there is only One, then whatever is has to be an expression of that One. This leads to an awareness that whatever has transpired in our lives is perfect even though we may not understand it or it may have caused us great pain.

Fifth, **we actually see the energy world as it is**, rather than seeing only the abstracted images of the energy world in our psyches. This perception integrates all the others, because we see that the world is a woven tapestry of energy patterns, none of which can really be separated from the others. All are affected by all others.

Each contributes to the state of all others. We actually *see* that this is One World, and that that world is a vast energy system or field. The one field is composed of fields within fields within fields.

These intuitive perceptions completely turn our consciousness inside out or upside down. We realize that we must make a return journey through the chakras to turn the mirrors upward to reflect the Light of truth rather than our own state of consciousness. We must re-align our thinking, our feeling, and our acting to reflect the truth of who we are. (See Chapter Ten.)

As we said on page 169, this is the energy of the Science Ray moving through us, motivating us to understand how we function and then to put that new understanding into practice through our personal expression in the world.

Moon in Cancer

In esoteric astrology, the **Moon in Cancer** symbolizes the final stage of the lunar phase of the individualizing process and corresponds to the opening of the Third Eye Chakra. The moon, of course, shines by reflected light, and the Third Eye Chakra is part of the structure of the human psyche, which functions entirely by reflection. Thus the use of the **Moon**, which shines by reflected light, as a symbol for the quickening of the forces in the Third Eye Center tells us that the fundamental nature of the psyche has not changed. That is, the psyche still functions by reflection.

> However, when we enter this phase of the awakening a very important shift in orientation occurs, from outer to inner perception.
>
> The faculty of consciousness that is awakened in the Third Eye Chakra is intuitive awareness. The key words for **Cancer** are "**I feel.**" We are not yet functioning in direct perception, but we are learning to see a much clearer reflection of reality. We begin to have a feeling for what it will be like to function directly in the Christ consciousness. We see that we are building a lighted house in which to dwell.

How Shall We Understand the Force that Is Released in These Experiences of Awakening?

Perhaps the most fundamental understanding we need to develop is that our consciousness of the power at work throughout the cosmos is expanding. That expansion usually takes the form of the discovery that there are many additional functions available to us than we were aware of prior to the expansion.

Let us return to our house metaphor. Remember when we spoke, back in Chapter Three, about rewiring the House of Self so that more voltage could be brought in? That analogy holds true. The corollary is that now that greater power is available in the House of Self, we can use appliances that require much higher voltage. So when we begin to see into the past or the future, it is as if we have just installed a new appliance like a high definition television set with a satellite dish. We are able to see programs that were not available to us before, and to see them in greater clarity.

With the capacity of the Third Eye Chakra awakened, we become able to observe all the functions of the psyche and to understand them. Thus we are able to take conscious control of the power flowing into the House of Self. We do that by realizing that the force flows into these various faculties or activities in the chakras, but the force can also be turned off. So, for instance, if you are seeing things that haven't happened yet and that is disturbing to you, all you have to do is redirect the energy so that it no longer empowers that particular activity. That is like unplugging an appliance or turning off a light switch.

Or suppose, in the Throat Chakra, a stream of memories keeps running across your mental screen and you do not want to entertain those memories. You can "switch channels," directing the mind to think about something else, thus utilizing the energy in the way you choose. Or you can turn the "set" off by directing the Throat Chakra energies up into the Third Eye or the Crown Center, or down into the Heart Chakra.

What we need to understand is that more power is available to us and that we are aware of more functions to be activated in each of the chakras. With that new awareness comes the responsibility to take charge of the energy we use. We can turn it on and off. We can increase it by focusing our attention and using conscious breathing. We can decrease it by slowing down our breathing and exhaling more than we inhale. We can redirect the energy from one activity or expression to another. And when we are not engaged in purposeful and creative expression of our heightened power resources, we can direct them into the Crown Chakra where they will nurture our further unfolding.

> **Ways to Practice:**
>
> 1. **As you continue to practice the full breath, sit quietly with your spine erect. Breathe in and out through the center of your forehead, just between and above your eyebrows.** Practice discerning the qualities that characterize the Third Eye Chakra frequencies.
>
> 2. **As you practice lifting energy on the breath from one chakra to the next, add the Third Eye Chakra to the list.** Lift the energies from the Throat Chakra into the Third Eye and see if you can discern the difference in the qualities of the energy.
>
> 3. **On the breath, practice opening and closing the Third Eye Chakra.**
>
> 4. **Practice meditation.** Hold a question in your consciousness as you sit quietly, doing your full breathing and focusing your attention in the Third Eye Chakra. Hold your attention in the Third Eye Center. Continue your steady, full breath. Hold your question as your one thought. And wait, in abundant expectancy. The answer will come, if not today, then tomorrow. Be patient and hold your focus.

5. Pay attention when you have an urge to know. Pursue it actively through study, research, analysis, observation, and experimentation. Be aware that this is the energy of the Science Ray motivating you. Cooperate with it.

6. Observe your thoughts. Notice that you live in a sea of thoughts. Begin to practice discrimination, allowing entrance to the House of Self only those thoughts that will make your internal space beautiful, nourishing, and life-giving.

7. Notice how often you register thoughts other people are sending to you.

8. Practice sending thoughts to others by holding in your circle of attention at the same time the thought and the person to whom you want to send it.

Notes:

10
Reorienting Ourselves: From Outer to Inner

Once the Third Eye Chakra opens, we discover how much there is to know about the energy world in which we live and how much we have yet to discover about ourselves. This sets in motion, or intensifies, a profound process of reorientation. Instead of looking outward to other people or to the truth as described by others, we use the light of our own experience as our guide. This is the powerful influence of the **Science Ray**, through the **Third Eye Chakra**, urging us to test everything against our own experience and to accept nothing as true solely because it is reported to us by another.

The strong influence of the Science Ray is reinforced by our incidents of intuitive awareness. Though those events revealed truth to us, we did not come to that truth firsthand. Instead we registered reflected perceptions in the Third Eye Chakra. Now we revisit the other four chakras of the personality to expand both our understanding of the truth we have perceived intuitively and our experience of the truth as we have come to know it through each of the other chakras.

We also seek to consciously reorient the energies of

each chakra so that they are directed upward toward the Crown Chakra rather than outward into the world around us. In other words, we take responsibility for *creating our own reality consciously, rather than living as if we have no control over our lives.*[1] We do this by relying only on our own experience of reality rather than projecting outward onto others the power to *make us* feel, think, believe, or do anything.

How Does Our Thinking Change?

As we reenter the Throat Chakra we develop the receptive, yin side of our thinking process. In the first stirrings of the energies in the Throat Chakra we sought to reorder the second story of our House of Self rather aggressively by throwing out old mental images, beliefs, world views, opinions, values, and understandings and bringing in new ideas gathered from authoritative sources different from the ones with which we were raised. We went "out" looking for new mental furnishings, so to speak, that seemed more expressive of our growing experience of life. It was a yang, active pursuit born of the initial fervor of our awakening consciousness.

The Throat Chakra partakes of both air and fire. The energy released in this chakra can be dry like air or exciting and illuminating like fire. In this new phase of awakening in the Throat Chakra, we breathe into the spaciousness of our own experience and take the time to

---

1. In this chapter you will find **The Love Principles** highlighted in bold italic. For further elaboration on these principles, see *The Love Principles,* by Arleen Lorrance, Scottsdale, AZ: Teleos Imprint, 2001.

find our own words and concepts to express what we are coming to know. We take the awareness that comes through perceptive cognition in the Throat Chakra frequencies and hold it in yin energy as we let it develop into a clear expression of our own intuition and frequency registration at the Third Eye level. We trust our own experience and we trust ourselves to be able to find the words and concepts to express what we know.

An example of this process from my own experience was the development of the method I call "Life As A Waking Dream." Recognizing that life is a waking dream is nothing new. Almost all the Wisdom Teachings describe life as we experience it in our ordinary human state of consciousness as a dream, and teachers today increasingly use the term "waking dream."

My unique contribution came in seeing that we could actually *use* these waking dreams to guide us in our process of awakening. We could *analyze* the waking dreams (the yang polarity of the awakening in the Throat Chakra) and meditate on the symbols (the yin polarity of the awakening in the Throat Chakra) in order to find the deeper meaning in our life experiences. I intuited (Third Eye Chakra) that our waking dreams (what we usually call "real life experiences") are actually symbolic modes of communication used by the Great Mother (the Great Yin) to teach us about life and guide us through it.

I was patient (yin) in my process of developing this method of interpreting life experiences. I invited twenty people to participate with me for a year in exploring the validity of my premise. This was to honor direct experience and to proceed in harmony with the Science Ray. As I guided our exploration, I looked only inward to find my way. I trusted my own intuition (Third Eye Chakra) and sought to capture in my thought processes (Throat

Chakra) what I registered intuitively.

The initial year of examining waking dreams proved that the method could be very useful. Consequently, I began to offer classes in which I taught the method, and for many years now people have found deeper meaning in their lives using this method.

I remember the discipline of those first years. Someone would ask me a question. If I could stay focused on the inner registry, with my thinking faculty acting as a receptor and reflector of what I was registering in Third Eye frequencies, then I could find words to express what I was intuiting/seeing/knowing. If for a moment I looked within my already developed thoughts and concepts for a way to answer the question, that is, into my memory, I was immediately lost. I had no referent for the answer. I had failed to look to the higher frequencies of registry and thus could not capture in my thought processes what I knew intuitively. In those moments I would just have to respond, "I'm sorry, I have lost the frequency. I cannot answer your question at this moment."

After seven years of guiding others in working with their waking dreams and of working with my own waking dreams, I wrote my method down in a book called *Life As A Waking Dream.*[2] I was thrilled with what I had to offer and wanted to give it wide distribution. I thought it was my most important contribution thus far. I found an agent and she submitted my manuscript to publishers.

What followed was a difficult but clear learning for me. Riverhead Books offered me a contract for my book and I signed it. Then I began working with the editor who was assigned to me. The editor was focused on

---

2. Riverhead Books, 1997.

"what the reader wants" rather than on what I had to offer. Whether she actually knew what the reader wants is irrelevant. What was relevant to my learning was that I gave over the power to this outer authority, as if I were still in need of approval from others. I accepted her judgment of what would communicate and what wouldn't. In the process, I agreed to eliminate from the manuscript what for me was the heart and soul of the method, namely, the wisdom on which it was based. Also eliminated were the exercises that invited readers to test the method out in their own experience.

I had violated my own knowing that I was to look within for direction, not without. Also, I knew that I was to find my own words to express what I had come to know through my own experience, not to rely on some outer authority for the form of that expression.

When the book came out, those who had worked with me over the seven years as I developed the method said, "This book lacks the life force of the work we have done." The fire had been put out. I made an effort to promote the book, and it sold a respectable number of copies. But in my heart I knew it was not my best; it was not fully expressive of the gift I could have given to the world. As a result, I suffered a creative depression for a year after the book was published. And when I emerged from the depression I vowed I would never again let an outer authority alter the form of what I had come to know through direct experience.

I believe this illustrates the lesson of this phase of the awakening process, which is to come to know through frequency registration and to unleash the power to find our own words and images to express our direct experience. In this phase we truly learn to think for ourselves without the support of outer authorities.

In fact, during this phase we question all authority and subject everything to the test of our own experience. We look for flexible mental structures that can be changed in the light of new evidence. We develop more expansive world views, constantly asking why and how. We engage with others in a back and forth dialog, *providing others with opportunities to give to us*[3] based on their experience. We communicate rather than pontificate.

We awaken a sense of self as the observer (some prefer the term "witness") with the mind as a helper, catching a reflection of what the observer sees, and thinking it through in the light of the big picture. If we observe that we feel trapped, for example, we then examine our immediate circumstances to determine what might be evoking the feeling. We then hold the feeling up to the light of our past experience, our understanding of the present circumstance, and our purposes and objectives within the situation. Only then do we ask ourselves whether we want to act on the feeling of being trapped, or whether we want to move that energy on the breath and activate another feeling that will be more likely to serve our overall intention.

We also observe our thought processes in order to use the mind more efficiently and effectively. In the aftermath of a situation such as the one described above, we will look back at the way we thought through what was transpiring within to determine whether we could have found clarity by a more direct mental route.

---

3. See *The Love Principles,* ibid.

Mercury in Gemini

Mercury in Gemini symbolizes this phase of our unfolding awareness in the Throat Chakra. **Gemini** is an air sign, whereas Virgo is a fire sign. The Throat Chakra partakes of both air and fire energies.

In this new phase of awakening in the Throat Chakra, we breathe into the spaciousness of our own experience and take the time to find our own words and concepts to express what we are coming to know. We take the awareness that comes through perceptive cognition in the Throat Chakra frequencies and hold it in yin energy as we let it develop into a clear expression of our own intuition and frequency registration at the Third Eye level. We trust our own experience and we trust ourselves to be able to find the words and concepts to express what we know.

This illustrates the lesson of the phase symbolized by Mercury in Gemini. **Mercury** represents communication "from the gods." The term "from the gods" refers to what we come to know through frequency registration. And Gemini represents the power to find our own words and images to express our direct experience. The key words for Gemini are **"I think."** In this phase we truly learn to think for ourselves without needing the support of outer authorities.

How Does Our Loving Change?

As we descend to the Heart Chakra, following the opening of the Third Eye Center, we recognize that in the first phase of our awakening in this chakra we were almost entirely focused on pouring out love to others. Yes, we were learning about balance, and about the wisdom to know when to give and when not to give. But the focus nevertheless was on the outer, on loving others. Now we learn to balance the flow of love between the outer and the inner.

When the Heart Chakra was first activated, we awakened to a love of all of Life and an exhilarating joy at all the love there was to give. Now we return to humanness, to giving with wisdom out of an understanding of Life Itself, of human nature, and of self. We no longer see love of self as contradictory to the love of others. We *receive ourselves, as well as all others, as beautiful exactly as we are*,[4] knowing that we are all human. We recognize that we *are* love, and that we *are loved*. The universal and unconditional love is grounded in us. We realize that we *have* love; it can never be taken from us. We live and express that love all day everyday, everywhere, and in relation to everyone.

We continue to expand our capacity for unconditional and universal love. With our larger vision we are willing to expand our giving into the universal, well beyond the few to whom we may have tried to pour out our love in our first awakenings of the Heart Chakra. We recognize that there is *so much love to give* that there is no

---

4. Ibid.

limit to it. It cannot be confined to personal relationships without overwhelming others. Only by pouring it out to any and all persons we meet can we be true channels for this dynamic force.

We develop more patience for the life process in all its complexity. We recognize that we are not part of some vast project to remodel personalities and reconstruct the world around us; rather, everything is perfect just as it is in the grand scheme of things. We focus in on the motivating urges that we are registering in our own consciousness and we *receive ourselves as beautiful* in responding to those in the most faithful way we can.

We become more at home in the material world. Early impressions of the spiritual life often include images of saintly beings who deny their bodies with fasting, who renounce worldly possessions, and who resolve all their problems through prayer and meditation. As we revisit the Heart Chakra in the light of all that is revealed to us in the Third Eye Chakra, we recognize that the physical realm is a manifestation of higher frequencies of energy. Therefore, to become a spiritual master is to be able to live consciously and creatively in and through physical form.

We become more earthy, learning to delight in nature and in human contributions to creativity through technical, mechanical, architectural, industrial, artistic, and other avenues of expression that contribute to our style of living. We see the beauty in all things as well as in all persons.

We no longer see sensuality and sexuality as forces that need to be transmuted. Instead, we recognize that the primal creative force expresses through sexuality, and that the senses make it possible for us to enjoy the fruits of all creativity.

In these and many other ways we see the beauty of the lower chakras. In so doing, we redeem physical and emotional expression and bring them into the service of unconditional love.

In this phase of our awakening in the Heart Center, we no longer see a contradiction between being human and being divine. Having seen intuitively in the Third Eye Center that All is One, it is easier to recognize that *the One manifests fully as each one.* We consciously cultivate such qualities as loving kindness, compassion, and unconditional, universal love to prepare the way for the Christ Force, the Life Force Itself, to take up permanent residence in our own Heart Centers after the union of the yin and yang forces that culminates the solar phase of unfolding (see Chapter Twelve).

Venus in Taurus

In esoteric astrology, the symbols for this phase of the Heart Chakra opening are **Venus in Taurus**. **Venus** continues to represent our capacity for unconditional and universal love, but in the sign of **Taurus** that love becomes much more practical. We recognize that we *are* love, and we *are loved*. The universal and unconditional love is grounded in us. The key words for Taurus are "**I have**" and what we realize we have is love. It can never again be taken from us.

In the stages symbolized by Venus in Li-

> bra we were awakened to a love of all of Life and an exhilarating joy at all the love there was to give. Now, in the phase represented by Venus in Taurus, we return to humanness, to giving with the wisdom and understanding of Life Itself, of human nature, and of self. We no longer see love of self as contradictory to the love of others. We *receive ourselves as beautiful as well as all others*, knowing that we are all human.

Letting Go of Denial and Daring to Be Who We Are

Receiving ourselves as beautiful exactly as we are makes it much easier to reenter the Solar Plexus Chakra with the intention to bring into consciousness those energies that flared up uncontrollably in the initial phases of the awakening forces there. The warlike energies of the Solar Plexus that made us willing to fight for what we desire and to protect what we already have are now transformed.

We are driven by the urge, awakened by the Harmony Ray, to establish total harmony in our own nature, and to bring the Solar Plexus energies into alignment with the universal love of the Heart Chakra and the comprehensive perspective of the Throat and Third Eye Chakras. We are willing now to give up denial, that is, the refusal to see things as they really are. We let go of beliefs, desires, and ways of being that were cultivated in our own psyches, often with the full support of the group psyches in which we were integrated, choosing instead to respond in the moment to what is. We finally let go of the stories we have told ourselves to excuse our fear of, and refusal to be, our authentic selves.

Initially we were dealing with the turbulence of the psychic depths in which deep secrets were hidden and unrest was easily aroused. Now we dive deep into the waters and bring up into the air, into the light of greater awareness, not only any remaining hidden fears and repressed desires, but also any treasures still buried due to a diminished sense of self.

When we looked outside of ourselves for our fulfillment, believing that others could make us whole, we also kept buried talents and skills that had been developed in other lifetimes, that we felt unworthy to express through our current personalities. Now, in the light of the new perceptions of ourselves as loved and as integral to the life process, we begin to claim those treasures as our own and to dare to give them expression. We gain our strength from within, rather than from without. We now **view any problems that arise as opportunities**[5] for our personal growth and development.

I know a woman who, when she entered this phase, dared to reveal the many profound insights she had gained over the years through her meditation. In earlier stages of her unfolding, she had withdrawn each time someone questioned any aspect of what she had come to see and to know. There was a voice inside that kept saying, "Who do you think you are?" One day she realized, "I am who I am. I have as much right as anyone to reveal what I know." On that day she uncovered her talent

---

5. Ibid.

for writing and painting. She not only gave words to her growing insight into the nature of reality, but she was able to illustrate her insights with magnificent paintings. She began to share her writings and paintings in the small community where she lived, and eventually her works became more widely known. She had emerged into the light of day, no longer hiding her talents in the shadow of her fears.

This woman is a good example of the shift that comes when we reenter the Solar Plexus and become a Warrior for our own wisdom and self-expression. We function with a fire that burns within and results in a radiance that cannot be dimmed by the responses of others. Like the sun, we simply radiate the life force that burns within us. Whoever is willing to open to that energy will be quickened by it.

At this stage of our awakening, our individualizing process becomes established on the feeling level. We are no longer dependent on others for the fulfillment of our needs and desires, or to make us whole, or to give us approval. We know "I am whole." We are willing to go it alone in our lives if we need to. We initiate rather than react and are more likely to have a following than to need company.

We have found the freedom and satisfaction of both knowing and feeling **"I Am."** In this knowing, we release the power of the life force in feelings such as confidence, happiness, boldness, and assertiveness.

Mars in Aries

Receiving ourselves as beautiful exactly as we are makes it much easier to reenter the Solar Plexus with the intention of bringing into consciousness those energies that, in the phase symbolized by Mars in Scorpio, flared up uncontrollably. This new phase of awakening in the Solar Plexus is represented **by Mars in the sign of Aries**. Scorpio is a water sign and represented the turbulence of the psychic depths in which deep secrets are hidden and unrest is easily aroused. But **Aries** is an air sign and symbolizes the movement to dive deep into the waters and bring up into the air, into the light of greater awareness, not only the hidden fears and repressed desires, but also the treasures that have been buried due to a diminished sense of self.

The key words of Aries are **"I am."** This represents the fact that our individualizing process is becoming established on the feeling level. We are no longer dependent on others for the fulfillment of our needs and desires, or to make us whole. We now know "I am whole." We are willing to go it alone in our lives if we need to. We now initiate rather than reacting and are more likely to have a following than to need company.

We have found the freedom and satisfaction of both knowing and feeling "I am."

Generation Is Transmuted into Regeneration

As we reenter the Generative Chakra, we are profoundly aware that the energies we previously expended pursuing others must be redirected. We awaken the yin polarity of this very active chakra, and the energies of the Devotional Ray are directed into the service of the Heart Center and the higher frequencies of the Third Eye Chakra.

It is at this stage that we realize we have the power to give life to the new self symbolized by the Christ child. That new self was first "born" in the Generative Chakra, but at a time when we didn't understand the inner process of our awakening. Now we can see that the energies of the Generative Chakra can be used almost entirely for our inner development.

The process of **generation** has to do with giving birth to physical forms. Specifically, it has to do with perpetuating the human race through reproduction so that individuals can have the opportunity to reach the regenerative phase of their development. **Regeneration is about giving new life to what already has form.** It is the spiritual rebirth that is spoken of in almost all religious traditions.

At this stage of our awakening, we no longer simply "believe" in the spiritual life, we have come to *know* it. It has been revealed to us through our own experience. We have become oriented to an inner, unseen reality that has become more real to us than the outer, objective reality that absorbed all our time and attention before the onset of the process of awakening.

In the Generative Chakra, we now direct our creative energies into *being the change we want to see hap-*

pen in the world, rather than trying to change anyone else.[6] We are yin, or receptive, to the higher frequencies of energy in our own fields, and we have directed our creative forces into the service of those higher frequencies. We have become spiritual rather than religious. We have developed a direct relationship with the higher energy rather than a codified, conventional relationship through the constructs called beliefs and creeds. We now recognize that we are esoteric rather than exoteric, psychic rather than objective. We discover that we learn well in our sleep, as our psyches go to inner classrooms for instruction in the Wisdom.

We have now prepared the way for the Christos Force to take its seat in our personalities. Our psyches have been cleansed and they are reoriented to the inner. We hold our attention focused in the highest frequencies we can register, and we watch and wait for the fire to descend.

Neptune in Pisces

The sign of **Pisces** represents the culmination of the lunar phase of our unfolding. At last we are prepared to fully manifest spirit. Not only do we consciously incarnate our own spiritual nature and understanding, but we recognize that the Kingdom of Heaven (the Kingdom of God) is here on earth. It is not something we have to leave our physical bodies to experience.

---

6. Ibid.

The discovery of **Neptune** in 1846 coincided with the discovery of anesthetics and hypnotism. Neptune is associated with deception, drugs, extreme sensitivity, spirituality, religions, psychic phenomena and altered mental states, among other things.

In esoteric astrology, **Neptune in Pisces** symbolizes the final dissolution of all illusions about the physical world as objective to us or separate from us. The key words of Pisces, **"I believe,"** are transmuted into **"I reveal,"** for we recognize now that in everything we do and say and are we reveal the true nature of the One Self expressing through us.

Ways to Practice:
1. **When you interact with others, breathe into the Throat Chakra before speaking.** Imagine that your thinking is being illumined from above. Take the time to find your own words and concepts to express what you are coming to know. Do not go "out" to wonder what the other person will think or understand. Seek to satisfy yourself that you have done the best you can in that moment to say what *you* want to say.

2. Practice *receiving all people as beautiful exactly as they are*, including yourself, in all situations by breathing through the Heart Chakra on both the inhale and the exhale.

3. **In all circumstances, dare to be yourself fully, truthfully, unapologetically.**

4. **Live each day in the consciousness that you are a spiritual being fully integrated in an energy world.** Let Light shine through you in joy and freedom.

11
From Air to Fire

By now I hope you have begun to hold in your awareness the fact that there is a difference between the structure of the individual that we recognize with our objective consciousness and the actual structure of the individual in the energy world. On the objective level, before we begin the process of awakening, we speak of a body, emotions, mind, and a higher self, or spirit. We relate all aspects of the individual to the body. We associate the emotions with the gut, the mind with the head, and the spirit with the heart. We are so identified with the body on the objective level that many people think that when the body dies, the individual ceases to be.

However, as we awaken, we discover that the structure of the individual in the energy world is differently delineated and far more dynamic. An autonomous field of energy is composed of seven vortices of energy called chakras. Five of the chakras channel energy into what we recognize in objective consciousness as the body and psyche. The other two chakras are the polarities of the autonomous field. They hold, between them, the lines of force on which the seemingly objective body and psyche take form. Energy flows through each of these chakras and intermingles throughout the individual's field.

This autonomous field of energy is the House of

Self that emerges out of the cosmic process to provide a structure within which the individual can become conscious of self. (See Illustration #11) The emergence of this House of Self is part of the entire sweep of the cosmic process that we often call creation or evolution. In other words, we are integrated in the cosmic process, an essential part of the whole. We did not set our own growth process into motion and the design of the structure was not ours to determine or choose. The cosmic process working through the human group energy field provided the structure of the House of Self.

However, *consciousness* of the structure and of self defines the individual. As Cynthia Bourgeault puts it (see page 164), we "tease the shape of the divine [as it emerges] out of the eternal and into the now." Everything already is, in its perfection (see page 178), but we are like creative midwives who intuit "the new patterns as they arise in the imaginal and [help] birth them into form."[1] We are a vital part of the process of *becoming*, through which the potential of the Original One is brought into form and expression. And we are essential to the awakening that enables the Original One to come to know Itself.

As our consciousness expands, we know more and more aspects of the One Self, and through us, that One Self (which can be called God) is awakening. In other words, each field of energy can be likened to a cell in the body of the One Self. As the One Self awakens from the sleep that we call subconsciousness, It becomes aware of Itself one cell at a time. The One Self discovers that It *is* each one of those cells. It identifies with the cell. In ef-

---

1. Cynthia Bourgeault, *The Wisdom Way of Knowing,* pages 82 and 83.

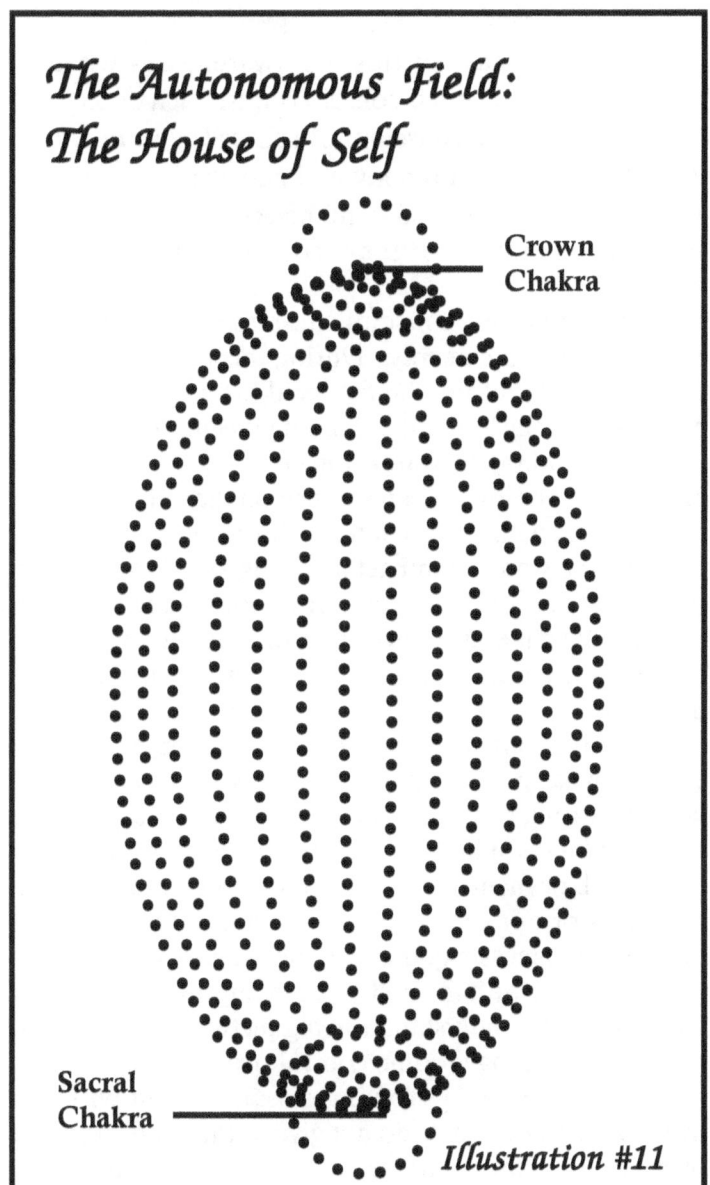

Illustration #11

fect, It says to Itself, "I *am* this cell."

The first phase of this self-awareness is what we have called objective self-consciousness. Each of us *is* the One Self becoming conscious of self *as body and personality*. We identify with body and personality, or psyche. We think we *are* the body and personality. We see ourselves as separate from the world around us and from other persons.

Objective self-consciousness requires a minimal amount of cosmic energy. During this phase of our development, therefore, the five chakras empowering the body and psyche are only minimally open. If we were to liken the chakras to water faucets, it is as if the water pressure is very low. When we turn on the faucet, the water flows out without much force. Moreover, it is difficult to direct the water to impact anything at a distance from the faucet. In a similar fashion, enough energy flows through the chakras to enable us to function as persons, but our impact on others and on the world around us is minimal.

In time our psyches become more organized. We develop what psychologists call strong egos. That is, we develop strong senses of self, clear boundaries, and the ability to function in the world independent of monetary, emotional, or mental support from family or other representatives of our socializing communities. At that point our consciousness expands so that we are no longer totally identified with the body. A longing awakens in us to know more, to understand the big picture of things, and to learn how to have some control over our lives. At the same time, we feel a growing dissatisfaction with our lives. Our achievements do not give us the enduring sense of accomplishment and security that we had hoped to find.

When that occurs, the water pressure increases, to return to the analogy of the faucets, and the greater force flowing through the chakras initiates a new growth spurt in our consciousness. We have described that growth spurt as the lunar cycle of the awakening process.

How Can We Summarize the Lunar Cycle?

As greater force is released in our psyches, we awaken new faculties of consciousness. The power of the Devotional Ray flowing through the Generative Chakra motivates us strongly to be of service to the family, tribe, and nation to which we are born. A powerful devotional energy is released that awakens in us the urge to give our lives meaning by serving others. We dedicate ourselves to causes that, in our view, will benefit family, tribe, and nation. Our motivations are not selfless or universal in scope. Rather, we seek to direct the increased power of the Generative Chakra into creativity that will benefit those who are closest to us and with whom we are most identified. And because more force is flowing through us, we have a greater impact on other people and on the world around us. We become leaders and reality shapers in one form or another within the circles of our close associations.

When more force is released in the Solar Plexus Chakra, our devotion becomes even more personal. We want not only to serve those closest to us but also to fulfill our own desires. Motivated by the Harmony Ray, we want to be at peace within ourselves and with others, but not at the expense of what we value most. In fact, we are willing to fight for what we want and what we believe is rightfully ours.

When the Heart Chakra energies are increased, a

pronounced shift occurs in our consciousness. Our awareness expands to the larger world community to which we belong and to persons in our more immediate surroundings who are not part of our personal life. A strong urge to love all these people is awakened in us by the Love-Wisdom Ray, and we find we cannot love universally and unconditionally if we cling to our personal values and world-views. We begin to register the voice of inner direction and to acknowledge that we must lift ourselves up out of the group energy fields in which we were raised.

In the Throat Chakra the increased energy flow of the Ceremonial Ray empowers us to give new order to our mental, or private, worlds. We learn to communicate more powerfully our convictions and beliefs. We become spokespersons for the energy reality we begin to comprehend, and we strive to make our daily lives an outward representation of the sacredness of that understanding.

The increased energy released in the Third Eye Chakra during the lunar phase broadens our vision to include the ability to see beyond the time- and space-bound reality of objective consciousness. It also awakens our perceptive cognition so that we understand deeper truths about reality. Our intuition grows stronger and more reliable, and the Science Ray quickens our curiosity so that our quest for knowledge and understanding is unending.

Have We Learned to Distinguish Between Force and Form?

The force or power that motivates a given chakra does not determine the form of expression we give to that force. The choices we make, whether unconsciously or consciously, determine the forms of expression. The force is like electricity, invisible to our senses, yet available for our use. The forms of expression are like the appliances that are powered by electricity (a desk lamp, a space heater, a motor, etc.)

In the Generative Chakra, for example, one of the forms of expression of the creative force carried on the Devotional Ray is sexual intercourse. However, a multitude of other forms are expressions of that same creative energy: sports activities, dance, playing musical instruments, potting, sculpting, painting and other expressive arts, martial arts, therapeutic massage, cosmetology, gardening, carpentry, and many other physical manifestations of creativity.

In the Solar Plexus the same creative force, carried on the Harmony Ray, gives rise to a full spectrum of feeling forms, from anger to contentment, sadness to happiness, resentment to appreciation, etc., and to a diversity of forms of expression in words, sounds, tears, laughter, sighs, gasps, and so forth.

The force flowing through a given chakra does not determine the form of expression it will take. The emerging individual decides that through the choices he/she makes.

If we have met the challenge of the lunar phase of our awakening, therefore, we have learned to differentiate between the force and the energy center, the force and the quality of that force, the force and the activity it motivates, and the force and our individual states of consciousness. There is only one universal creative force, and it is with that creative force that we work as we learn to be co-creators.

During the lunar phase of our awakening we have learned to consciously tap the power that motivates everything and to control and direct it through the force centers and into the higher triad: the Throat, Third Eye, and Crown Chakras. By directing the creative force through the chakras we have developed faculties of consciousness that serve our self-expression not only during the lunar phase, but also during the solar cycle that follows, after the Christos Force is released more fully in us.

Some of the faculties of consciousness we have developed (see page 211) are attention, creativity, sensitivity, courage, perseverance, generosity of spirit, compassion, unconditional love, forgiveness, discernment, reason, humility, flexibility, perception, and understanding.

These faculties of consciousness are built **by reflection** during the lunar cycle. We reflect the qualities and characteristics of the people with whom we keep close company, and we are drawn to people who function in the frequencies that are in harmony with our current phase of unfolding.

As we change and grow, our companions also change and we are drawn into new groups and associations. If the company we keep has developed higher faculties of functioning, we will tend to learn those faculties by reflection and imitation. Of course the same is true if we associate with people who are less developed than we are. We will tend to devolve rather than evolve in their presence. Thus we have learned to choose our companions wisely and to associate with groups in which we are likely to meet persons who model the qualities of being that we seek to cultivate in ourselves.

We have also developed our faculties of consciousness **through action and reaction**. Each time we express ourselves (take action) we get a response, and that reaction gives us information that tells us whether or not our action was aligned with our intention. As the data from reactions accumulates and we make new choices based

Faculties of Consciousness
Developed during the Process of Awakening

Attention: the capacity to sustain a focus and thus to direct the flow of force
Creativity: the ability to bring things into physical manifestation
Sensitivity: the awareness of frequency registration
Courage: the willingness to take action according to consciously chosen purposes and objectives, that is, consciously set intentions
Perseverance: the capacity to complete activities set in motion
Generosity of Spirit: eagerness to give of oneself wisely
Compassion: a dispassionate sensitivity that feels for and with another without becoming identified with them
Unconditional Love: the eagerness to give to others without asking anything in return
Forgiveness: the ability to release energetic ties even though an injustice has been done to self or a loved one
Discernment: the capacity to make sound judgments based on clear insight and accurate discrimination of the facts
Reason: the ability to apply to the challenges of everyday living a proper understanding of the nature of the universe and the laws at work within it, of the nature of humanity and our place within the universe, and of the principles of the Wisdom
Humility: an aptitude for seeing things in their proper perspective, including self
Flexibility: the skill of adapting to changing circumstances and unexpected happenings
Perception: the ability to see things as they are in the energy world
Understanding: adeptness in applying the Wisdom Teachings to one's everyday life and the persons and events in it

on it and on our chosen objectives, we build our faculties of consciousness.

After we have turned our attention inward and upward to catch reflections of Light from the Crown Chakra during the lunar cycle, we also awaken to new possibilities through this inner seeing rather than looking outward for examples or confirmation.

Thus the process of remodeling and rebuilding the House of Self has continued throughout the lunar phase of our unfolding.

Making Straight the Way

Once the five force centers of the psyche have been energized and opened, they function as one center, blended and synthesized. The personality becomes a functional, integrated unit of consciousness through which the awakening power to be conscious can direct force and give expression to self, activating the various faculties (abilities or powers) of consciousness.

All these changes are necessary to prepare for what is often called the baptism by fire that will arise from the Sacral Chakra and descend through the Crown Chakra when the two polarities of our autonomous fields unite.

A new axis of energy opens in the energetic structure of the individual after the lunar phase is complete. The alignment of the **Sacral and Crown Chakra** energies expands the functional activities of the individual to include a direct registry of the **Activity Ray**, pouring through the Sacral Chakra, and of the **Will Ray** showering through the Crown Chakra. The energetic structure expands, and so does the individual's capacity for expression in the world. (See Illustration #11, page 205.)

The Will Ray registers in our consciousness as a

powerful motivation to function in the world with purpose and direction. We experience it as a driving force that moves everything by its quiet, still energy. To experience the force of the Will Ray is to be on fire with purpose. We move about in the world with a quiet knowing of what is wanted of us, with certainty, and with steadfastness of purpose. We are self-reliant, and others often look to us as mentors, teachers, and guides. We have enough life experience to respond to such invitations with both humility and generosity of spirit. We recognize that *choice is the life process.*[2]

The Activity Ray, pouring through the Sacral Chakra, is pure energy not yet configured into form. In our consciousness it registers as potential, and we recognize that anything is possible. We live in *abundant expectancy, but with no specific expectations.*[3] A penetrative and interpretative mental power is awakened in us. In other words, the Activity Ray motivates us to understand the principles behind creativity, to recognize what is needed to fulfill our purpose, to formulate plans, and to gather materials for the actualization of potential. No detail is too small to capture our attention. We become very adaptable in order to serve the higher Will. We prepare the ideational and energetic ground out of which material form will eventually emerge. Responsive to the Will Ray, the fire of creative activity rises up in us and illumines the whole self.

In the early stages of our awakening, we looked at the basement of the House of Self as primarily a foundation for the building that would stand above ground. It represented our total integration in the human energy

---

2. Lorrance, *The Love Principles.*
3. Ibid.

field, which is held by the larger fields out of which it emerged: the elemental, mineral, plant, and animal fields. The basement was also used to represent subconsciousness, universal unconsciousness, or the collective unconscious. As such it symbolized all the functions of consciousness that developed prior to our human self-consciousness.

We also recognized the physical body as a symbol similar to the basement, since it epitomizes the evolutionary process and provides us with the foundation for building an autonomous field. And in Chapter Four we talked about cleaning out the basement, making reference primarily to the body and our need to gain freedom from addictions and to restore health and balance to the body.

At the end of the lunar cycle we return metaphorically to the basement of the House of Self. Recognizing that during the solar cycle fire will course between the Sacral Chakra and the Crown Chakra, destroying anything that cannot be utilized in fulfilling the Will, we revisit the Sacral Chakra consciously.

The basement represents our subconscious functioning. Therefore, all our habit patterns are motivated and regulated from within the Sacral Chakra energies. If there are lessons we have yet to learn, they will be activated here, and we need to bring those lessons into our consciousness.

Habit patterns serve us well. They make it possible for us to accomplish more in a day than just the daily maintenance chores. Any change in our daily routine makes that amply clear. For example, I do forty to forty-five minutes of stretching and exercising at the beginning of each day. I do the same routine each morning, and I can go through it without giving it much thought, even though I give it my attention. However, when I travel, I have to focus very hard to remember the routine without the cues I get from my home environment. Because I start in one part of the room and move to the wall, the door, the chair, the doorway, and back to the floor, the stretches and exercises just seem to fall into place when I am at home. In a strange environment I have to consciously remember each segment of the routine and then find a place to do it. It takes me a lot longer and I often forget parts of the routine.

Or I think of the pattern of using the keyboard at my computer. As long as my subconscious is finding the keys on the keyboard, I can focus on what I am writing. But if for any reason I have to look at the keyboard to find the keys I need and want, my time is doubled or tripled. I have to slow down so I can do consciously what the pattern held in the subconscious can do much more efficiently.

So patterns are very helpful. However they can also enslave us if we want to replace the pattern with something that supports our current stage of development. I remember that when I committed myself to learn to live in unconditional love, back in 1970, I had a habit of making sarcastic remarks. Usually they made people laugh, but there was a mean spirit underneath them and I knew that the sarcasm had to go. It took a great deal of vigilant self-awareness to catch myself before a sarcastic remark was formed and to find something kind or understanding to say instead. It was not nearly as much fun for my personality. Not only did I give up the satisfaction of making others laugh (usually at the expense of someone else), but I also had to accept the fact that my friends would often groan or disagree with the positive comment I had made instead.

216   THE HOUSE OF SELF

This example illustrates one of the most common experiences people have when they return to the Sacral Chakra with conscious awareness at the end of the lunar phase of the awakening process. There is a tug of war between the frequencies of and above the Heart Chakra and the frequencies of the Solar Plexus, Generative and Sacral Chakras. Those qualities and patterns that are not in harmony with the higher frequencies of functioning will have to be transformed, and such changes are often not easy to make.

During this transition from the lunar to the solar phase of the individualizing process, we learn to stand firmly in the energies of the Heart Chakra, knowing that the personality, which is itself just a bundle of characteristic ways of behaving, cannot change patterns. We need to identify as much as possible with the higher self, the frequencies of Heart Chakra and above, and lift the forces of the lower chakras into the Heart Chakra where they can be balanced out. Anything from the past that limits us or constricts us, such as unwritten rules that translate into shoulds, have tos, and can'ts, as well as ways of being in the world about which we have regrets or guilt, must be lifted up into the Heart Center and held there. Addictive patterns such as smoking, drinking, eating too much or too little; emotional patterns of manipulation, control or abuse, or of being a victim; fantasies and desires, must all be lifted up.

There is no need to think about how to transmute these patterns once we have lifted them into the Heart Center. The frequencies of the Heart Chakra will do the work. We need only be mentally still and *feel* the power as these patterns fall apart from lack of attention and focus. We remain totally in the here and now, neither fighting with them nor feeding them with our attention. We focus only on the Heart Center; on the presence and power we feel when we are focused there. We remember, "I am the power to be conscious and I do not choose to direct power into those activities." And we have *patience.* The Heart Center forces will do the work of disintegrating those patterns so that the energy can be used again to build the new.

At this stage in our awakening, we find that our experiences will teach us all we need to know about the past and how it limits us. There may be old affinities and rapports that continue to have a hold on us. If so, those persons (or others like them) will come back into our lives and we will have an opportunity to look into the mirror of those relationships to discover how our own patterns of behavior and feeling hold us bound there. Whatever is in our outer life that appears to be out of harmony with the new we have been building and establishing in our lives, is a reflection of something within us. We can look into those mirrors to discover what we need to transmute.

In the tug of war between the higher and lower frequencies of our field, we keep being pulled down into a struggle with the past: old patterns, old habits, old relational dynamics. It is *very* hard to put up with because of all the work we have done to prepare ourselves for the beauty of the union of the yin and yang forces. However, in those previous efforts we learned to focus on our purpose and objectives, to hold our intentions constant, to focus our attention in the here and now, to speak the truth of what we have come to know, to use chants and toning to clear and organize our energies, to direct our forces, and to trust what we have come to know through our own experiences. (See chart on page 219.)

We can put all of these skills to work for us during

this tug of war, knowing that all the desires and wants of the personality must now come into alignment with a desire for union within. We want to make straight the way that the fire of the Christos will follow between the Sacral and Crown Chakras.

Our relationships change. Some people drop out of our lives. Others change alongside us. We may find new friends and new group associations to support us as we change. No one makes these transformational shifts in their life and consciousness without support from groups functioning in the higher frequencies to which we aspire.

Sometimes we refuse to go into the basement again, having had more than we want of it already. We deny that there is anything we are "hiding." In our conscious functioning we are not in fact hiding what is in the basement, but there may be a lot hidden there that we have not yet consciously uncovered. We may be ignorant of the larger pool of motivating forces at work in us. It is not that we are seeking to deceive others, or that we have ulterior motives. It may be that we are still ignorant of some of the content of our own House of Self.

Also during this transition we may have opportunities to teach. As we present what we know to others, they experience both what we know and what we don't yet know. They suggest, often by their questions, that there may be things we don't yet see. Or perhaps in our preparation to teach, we discover what we don't yet know and are moved to pursue it.

One of the most helpful things we can do during this transition is to set aside our conviction that we already know ourselves and that we understand how we function. **We can proceed instead with the conviction**

Consciousness Skills
Developed during the Lunar Phase

Remembering that we are living in an energy world

Remembering that our physical bodies are energy fields

Using the full breath, along with attention, to direct energies

Directing our forces through the chakras and from one chakra to another

Identifying the motivating forces of the different rays moving through the chakras

Distinguishing between force and form

Focusing on our purposes and objectives (what we want) as we express our creative energy

Holding our intentions constant

Focusing our attention in the here/now

Fulfilling our hidden desires

Loving unconditionally and universally

Speaking the truth of what we have come to know, and what we experience

Using chants and toning to clear and organize our energies

Trusting what we have come to know through our own experiences *that we know there is a lot we do not know and that we are on an adventure of discovery.*

It helps to have compassion for others and ourselves, and patience with the whole process. Constant return to the Heart Chakra will help us to sustain these qualities, and it will make it easier for us to receive support from others in our chosen groups, including frequency support from higher realms.

How Does Death Fit Into All of This?

The final limitation we must face consciously upon our return to the basement of the House of Self is death. In this regard, the basement becomes a symbol for the tomb. None of us escapes death, but as we come to the end of the lunar cycle of our awakening we discover that death is not an enemy, but rather a friend.

It is by facing death consciously that we learn to shift our sense of self firmly to identification with the power to be conscious. With the disintegration of each old habit pattern we die a small death. The decay and disintegration of the body are merely a more comprehensive manifestation of the same kind of dying. Death frees us from the constrictions of the form in which we have lived an entire lifetime in order that the energy be used for the building of a new energetic structure representative of the Self. Thus as we face death consciously, **we learn to welcome freedom from form** no matter how it presents itself to us.

In spite of how hard it seems, we learn to welcome the profound changes occurring within us and, as a reflection, in our outer lives. This is like welcoming active death. We look to the future, knowing that something entirely new is being built in us. The symbolism of the small child who was born in the manger (the Generative Chakra) shifts now to the mature adult who is sacrificed (crucified) in order to be resurrected into higher frequencies of functioning.

We recognize that any creative change requires the destruction of the old. If we are to be agents of the new, we must completely let go of the past. Change will occur in all aspects of the personality, and finally even in the body. We will be lifted up on the Sacral Chakra energies into the Crown Chakra where we will be born anew as a fully individualized being.

The Sacral Chakra power, called the kundalini (or Shakti) in the East, first moved up the ida and pingala channels, spiraling around the spinal cord like snakes uncoiling. In this polarized expression it entered each chakra, releasing more force for both yin and yang expressions. When those forces entered the Third Eye Center they freed the psyche to become a more perfect reflection of the higher frequency forces represented by the Crown Chakra.

In earlier stages of the evolution of humanity, the culmination of the lunar phase of awakening was so rare that those who had realized it were thought to be almost gods. In Egypt, for example, the Pharaohs were acknowledged as having completed the lunar phase of awakening. This was symbolized in statues of the Pharaohs by a serpent's head (or sometimes three serpent's heads) coming out of the center of the forehead. It wasn't until late in the history of the Pharaonic dynasties that Akhenaten (1370 BC) initiated the worship of the sun rather than the moon. This indicated the growing readiness of the group field to open to the solar phase of awakening.

In our time, astrologically called the Age of Aquarius (a 2,200 year period, approximately), the disintegration and destruction of the forms of the last 2,000 plus years are clearing the way for a radical change in the structures of societies. Belief (the key-word of the passing Age of Pisces) is being replaced by knowing (the keyword of the Age of Aquarius). The energies of this new age support the emergence of teamwork and partnerships rather than dictatorships and patriarchies. Since 1776, the United States of America has been seen as the prototype of the new political structures. The balance of power between three branches of government has been recognized as an expression of the higher triad that on the individual level is represented by the Throat, Third Eye and Crown Chakras.

The tug of war continues, in this twenty-first century. The old values of the patriarchy, which support the strong leader who will impose the new by force, still predominate. The values of the new collaborative forms of government (usually called democracy) struggle for support. The new values favor partnership and teamwork and trust the process of allowing the desire for the new to emerge from within the people who form the body politic of a given state or country. Many do not have the patience to allow the new values to work.

The same struggle goes on within each individual who is awakening, and the same shift of values needs to occur. The simple answers of the age of belief will not serve in this new age. We must learn to trust our own process of coming to know through experience, and we must trust the learning process of others.

Through cooperation rather than competition, collaboration rather than decree, and compromise rather than forced confrontation, we learn to live out the perception gained on the Third Eye level: that we are part of one whole and each and every individual contributes to the unfolding of the Larger Will. No one of us can grasp that Will in its entirety. We need each other to realize our full potential.

We are privileged to live in this time of transition, because we are living out the slow revelation of the Will through what we do. But we also must be willing to let go of the past and experience the pain of dying which precedes the new birth.

> ### Uranus in Aquarius
>
> As the solar phase of our journey begins, the energies of the **Sacral Chakra** are stirred to full and powerful activity. In Eastern lore, the Sacral energies are said to be like a coiled snake at the base of the spine. When this serpent is roused, the dynamic force that is released activates the baptism of fire and the movement into total identification with the Real Self.
>
> The sign of **Aquarius** is an apt symbol for the dramatic changes this shift brings about. We move beyond the laws of human beings into the higher law of the spirit, bringing about a virtual revolution in our lives. We are free from all that kept us from manifesting our full potential as reflections of the One Self. We become innovators who are alert to the new, curious about the unknown, and open-minded. We value team-work and search for partners with whom to cooperate as we seize opportunities to build a new world.

Uranus was only discovered in 1781. It was a precursor of all the radical changes that began in the 18th Century with the Industrial Revolution. It is sometimes seen as a higher octave of Mercury, and thus as a symbol for new forms of communication. **Uranus in Aquarius** represents the rapid changes we experience and express during this rising of the kundalini force. We become active agents of the new with the full recognition that that will bring about destruction of the old.

Ways to Practice:
1. Practice consciously expressing certain faculties of consciousness (such as those listed on page 211) in the course of each day.

2. Invite old habit patterns and qualities of being that are no longer in harmony with your state of development to come into your consciousness. Lift them, on the full breath, into the Heart Chakra to be transformed. Be mentally still and *feel* the power and presence of the Heart Chakra energies as they do the work of transformation for you.

3. Practice the consciousness skills listed on page 219 as you consciously make straight the way for the Christos fire.

4. Practice welcoming changes of form as preparations for the full release that comes with the process of dying.

THE HOUSE OF SELF

Unless the eye catch fire, the god will not be seen.

Unless the tongue catch fire, the god will not be named.

Unless the heart catch fire, the god will not be loved.

Unless the mind catch fire, the god will not be known.

— *William Blake*

12
The Work of Regeneration

Before humans begin the process of awakening, the power of the kundalini, the Mother Force, is used entirely for **generation.** That is, it is used to perpetuate life in the forms that emerged during the creating process. Most people are conscious of the force of generation as the sexual urge, which drives us to engage in intercourse with someone of the opposite sex so that we give birth to the next generation of humans. In the ethic of generation, "marriage" between a man and a woman was held sacred because only in the union of opposites could the species be kept alive. It was not until the end of the twentieth century that scientists learned to unite a sperm and an egg in a test tube, which makes it possible to perpetuate the species without the societal institution of marriage.

Once the process of awakening has begun, however, the power of the kundalini is used *within the individual* for **regeneration.** It is used to give birth to the individualized being in which the Christ Force directs all activity and self-expression. This is referred to in the Wisdom Teachings as the Inner Marriage. The polar opposite forces, the yin and yang, unite within to release the power of the individual, one who is whole and can never again be divided within self. The individual becomes one, and, in this inner union, the embodiment of the Original One. We were made in the image of that Original One. In the process of regeneration, we bring that image into conscious incarnation.

Beginning with the lunar phase of the awakening process, individuals undergo a progressive refinement of body, feelings, thoughts, actions, and loving. This refinement culminates in the release of the creative power of thinking and speaking, of perceptive cognition and intuitive awareness, which are the faculties of the higher triad, or the higher self.

The first development of the higher mind comes when the rising ida and pingala forces (the yin and yang) open the Throat Chakra. That enables us to express Christ consciousness. The development continues when the Third Eye Chakra is quickened, and it culminates when the Sacral Chakra energies rise up through the central channel of the spinal cord, the sushumna, and enter the Crown Chakra. It is in the Crown Chakra that the union of the yin and yang occurs, the Inner Marriage.

Once the Inner Marriage has occurred, the personality disappears into the individualized self. The lower triad (Sacral, Generative, and Solar Plexus Chakras) merge with the higher triad, or higher self (Heart, Throat and Third Eye Chakras). This unified self, which is an expression of the Christ force, becomes the manifested reflection of the Original One. The new House of Self is organized around the Heart Chakra frequency, which makes it possible for the individual to live in the physical world while functioning in the refined Christ consciousness. In traditional symbolism, the Christ (or Messiah) returns to Jerusalem (the Heart Chakra) to establish the Kingdom of God on earth.

The release of the kundalini into the sushumna seems to be a matter of maturation in the individual. Sometimes, but by no means always, it appears to be the direct result of concentration, contemplation, and/or meditation. Here is one account of that experience:

> Suddenly, with a roar like that of a waterfall, I felt a stream of liquid light entering my brain through the spinal cord. . . . The illumination grew brighter and brighter, the roaring louder. I experienced a rocking sensation and then felt myself slipping out of my body, entirely enveloped in a halo of light. It is impossible to describe the experience accurately. I felt the point of consciousness that was myself growing wider, surrounded by waves of light. It grew wider and wider, spreading outward while the body, normally the immediate object of its perception, appeared to have receded into the distance until I became entirely unconscious of it. I was now all consciousness, without any outline, without any idea of a corporeal appendage, without any feeling or sensation coming from the senses, immersed in a sea of light simultaneously conscious and aware of every point, spread out, as it were, in all directions without any barrier or material obstruction. I was no longer myself, or to be more accurate, no longer as I knew myself to be, a small point of awareness confined in a body, but instead was a vast circle of consciousness in which the body was but a point, bathed in light and in a state of exaltation and happiness impossible to describe.[1]

Gopi Krishna had prepared himself for such an experience by years of steady meditation practice, with

---

1. See Gopi Krishna's full account of this experience in *Kundalini: The Evolutionary Energy in Man,* Berkeley, CA: Shambala, 1971, page 11 and following.

strict focus and concentration. However, for some people the experience seems to come suddenly, without any warning, at any time or place, and with no apparent cause. Here is Richard Maurice Bucke's account of his awakening to what he called Cosmic Consciousness:

> All at once I found myself wrapped in a flame-colored cloud. For an instant I thought of fire, an immense conflagration somewhere close by in that great city; the next, I knew that the fire was within myself. Directly afterward there came upon me a sense of exultation, of immense joyousness accompanied or immediately followed by an intellectual illumination impossible to describe. Among other things, I did not merely come to believe, but I saw that the universe is not composed of dead matter, but is, on the contrary, a living Presence; I became conscious in myself of eternal life. It was not a conviction that I would have eternal life, but a consciousness that I possessed eternal life then; I saw that all men are immortal; that the cosmic order is such that without any peradventure all things work together for the good of each and all; that the foundation principle of the world, of all the worlds, is what we call love, and that the happiness of each and all is in the long run absolutely certain. . . .
>
> I saw with intense inward vision the atoms or molecules, of which seemingly the universe is composed – I know not whether material or spiritual – rearranging themselves, as the cosmos (in its continuous, everlasting life) passes from order to order. What joy when I saw there was no break in the chain – not a link left out – everything in its place and time. Worlds, systems, all blended into one harmonious whole.[2]

---

2. Richard Maurice Bucke in his book *Cosmic Consciousness,* New York: Arkana Books, 1991, page 9.

Or, consider this description by the Russian poet Alexander Pushkin:

The Prophet

>Athirst in spirit, through the gloom
>Of an unpeopled waste I blundered,
>And saw a six-winged seraph loom
>Where the two pathways met and sundered.
>He laid his fingers on my eyes:
>His touch lay soft as slumber lies —
>And like an eagle's, his crag shaken,
>Did my prophetic eyes awaken.
>Upon my ears his fingers fell
>And sound rose – stormy swell on swell:
>I heard the spheres revolving, chiming,
>The angels in their soaring sweep,
>The monsters moving in the deep,
>The green vine in the valley climbing.
>And from my mouth the seraph wrung
>Forth by its roots my sinful tongue;
>The evil things and vain it babbled
>His hand drew forth and so effaced,
>And the wise serpent's tongue he placed
>Between my lips with hand blood-dabbled;
>And with a sword he clove my breast,
>Plucked out the heart he made beat higher,
>And in my stricken bosom pressed
>Instead a coal of living fire.
>Upon the wastes, a lifeless clod
>I lay, and heard the voice of God:
>"Arise, oh, prophet, watch and hearken,
>And with my Will thy soul engird,
>Roam the gray seas, the roads that darken,
>And burn men's hearts with this, my Word.[3]

---

3. *The Poems, Prose and Plays of Alexander Pushkin,* New York, Modern Library, 1943, page 62.

Finally, read this description of Ramakrishna, an Indian saint who lived in the 19th Century:

> His religion meant ecstasy, his worship transcendental insight, his whole nature burnt day and night with the permanent fire and fever of a strange faith and feeling. His conversation was a ceaseless breaking forth of his inward fire and lasted for long hours.[4]

The changes that are set in motion by this response of the kundalini to the purified psyche, which is ready to embody the higher forces, are beyond the scope of this book, but I can point in the direction of the experience.

One of the indicators of the arousal of the kundalini is the awakening of the memory of past incarnations, the memory of the "earliest beginnings" before the lunar phase of the awakening process. This is what is often referred to in the Bible as the Judgment Day. The individual's entire past is reviewed and what can no longer serve is thrown into the fire of the energies of the Third Eye Center and the Crown Chakra to be consumed and returned to the earth from which it came. This is the final phase of the purification that began with the baptism by water, or the cleansing of the psyche, and culminates with the baptism by fire.

The kundalini force rises in the sushumna through each chakra and thus through each level of the psyche, body, feelings, and thinking, until it unites with the power to be conscious at the Crown Chakra.

When the yin and yang forces began their first journey through the ida and pingala channels, we, as regenerated individuals, were represented by the symbol of a

---

4. Bucke, page 313.

tiny child born in a manger. Along the way that infant Christ child was baptized with water and then lifted out of the waters of the psyche. We grew in stature as our knowledge and understanding of the nature of the Cosmos and of our place within it expanded. At the pinnacle of this initial ascent, our consciousness as emerging individuals underwent a transformation (symbolized in the New Testament by Jesus' experience on the Mount of Transfiguration). We became able to commune with higher beings and our consciousness was illumined with a cosmic perspective. We knew ourselves as one with all life.

But we also recognized that there was still work to do in cleansing our psyches. So the forces descended again through the chakras. (In the Biblical account, Jesus and his disciples descended from the Mount of Transfiguration to heal and teach.) We taught ourselves and healed ourselves in the light of this new seeing released in the Third Eye Center.

Finally, we returned to the Sacral Chakra, to the Mother, where we underwent the death of all identity with our bodies and psyches. (This death was symbolized by the crucifixion in the Bible.) After this baptism by fire, the crucified Christ was lifted up and the kundalini rose to the Crown Chakra, where recognition of the Mother of whom the child was born (the kundalini), and of the Father with whom the child is one (the power to be conscious), and of self as the Child of this Inner Marriage was released with enormous power within our consciousness as emerging individuals.

In what is sometimes referred to as the Second Coming of the Christ, the power of the unified consciousness reenters the Heart Chakra (symbolically represented by Jerusalem in the Biblical allegory) where it

234 THE HOUSE OF SELF

takes up permanent residence as Presence and the Power of Being.

The group field in which we function as individualized beings is available only in the energy world. It cannot be known or perceived by the objective mind and it is not made up of forms, as are the physical and astral levels. In Christ consciousness there is clear immediacy of knowing. It is the illumined Mind. It is *direct perception of the Will.*

The Christ Force is able to function in the higher mind while at the same time functioning at the physical, embodied level. When we are illumined by the Christ Force, we will *radiate* Light, not reflect it. We will be **co-creators** with the Cosmic Process. We will emanate energy that others can tap into and use, or that others can reflect.

Beings who function at this level of consciousness radiate out the frequencies that humans still in the lunar cycle register as thoughts, feelings, intuitions, insights, discoveries and revelations. In earlier periods these beings were thought of as gods. Now they are often referred to as masters, the hierarchy, enlightened beings, or avatars. These are merely terms used to identify the state of consciousness that we have here labeled the individualized being, or Christ consciousness.

Sun in Leo

The symbolic journey of the Sun from Capricorn through Sagittarius, Scorpio, Libra, and Virgo to the house of the **Sun in Leo** represents the rising of the kundalini through the sushumna, the hollow canal at the center of the spinal cord, from the **Sacral to the Crown Chakra**. There the Christos, born of the union of the Virgin Mother (kundalini) with the Father (the power to be conscious), is crowned King, as symbolized by **Leo**. In the sign of Leo the lion is represented as king; he symbolizes the strength, power, and courage of the "conqueror of beasts."

In the language of the esoteric astrology, the **Sun in Leo** symbolizes *the height of attainment as a human being.* It means the completion of the individualizing process. It also means the beginning of the next phase in which we function as fully conscious individuals, as the risen Sons of God.

The **Sun** is a self-generating power, giving light to all within its sphere of influence. It represents this phase of our unfolding in which we radiate Light from within, Light which those who are still in the lunar phase of development can reflect. We give off energy that others can tap into and use. We are self-generating in the sense that we are no longer dependent on group psyche identifications, or on knowing self as the personality. We are autonomous. We gain recognition as light-filled beings, but no longer need the recognition. We are bright, cheerful, radiant, happy beings. Extroverted, secure and optimistic.

What Is the Autonomous Field?

Once the Sacral and Crown Chakras are awakened, energy flows between them continuously, like the lines of force between the two poles of a magnetic field. (See Illustration #11, page 205.)These lines of force constitute an autonomous field, which means that the individual is no longer dependent on group psyche identifications, or on knowing self as the personality. Having experienced the inner marriage, the individual is whole within and consciously integrated in the energy reality. The individual's field is completely autonomous, or self-governing. This means that it can drop the body and psyche at any time and still maintain its identity.

These individuals find companionship in the frequency world. They are recognized as Light-filled beings, but they no longer need the recognition. On this human level, they manifest as bright, cheerful, radiant, and happy beings who direct their activities outward toward others. They are secure in their own knowing, in their ability to direct the forces, and in their identification with the Power-to-be-Conscious. They are optimistic about the outcome of the entire creating process and about each situation within it. Although the personality did not achieve this state of consciousness, it was an integral part of the becoming and it now perfectly reflects both the knowing and the willing.

We begin to reflect a lot of these characteristics in our personalities once we awaken the Heart Center energies and above. As we turn our forces upward to reflect the Light, we not only manifest these qualities with growing consistency, but we are able to talk about the

Noetic Mind and understand the concept of it, even though we have not yet experienced the Inner Marriage.

In this last stage of the process of unfolding, we, as individuals, are now one within and one with all, and we consciously assume direction and control of our further development. In other words, whereas with respect to the individualizing process we have reached maturity and have finished our developmental work, with regard to the next phase in the cosmic process of unfolding we are once again infants.

As fully conscious individuals we identify ourselves with our own fields. We are then called Logoi – reasons unto ourselves. We become Self-luminous as suns, and, our own fields being one with the solar field, we are now at home in any part of the solar system. We have completed adulthood as humans; but we have just been "born again" with respect to the second aspect of the Mother. Relative to the World-Mother, we are infants, beginning our higher evolution as *conscious* individualized Sons of God.[5]

And so it will be for us one day, if we continue to cooperate with the individualizing process already long at work within us.

---

5. Paraphrased from page 90, vol. 3 of Basic Teachings of the School of the Natural Order, by Vitvan. For a more complete presentation of the Purificatory Period (Lunar Phase) of the Individualizing Process, study Volume 3 of *The Natural Order Process: Basic Teachings of the School of the Natural Order,* by Vitvan (Baker, NV: School of the Natural Order, 1971).

Notes:

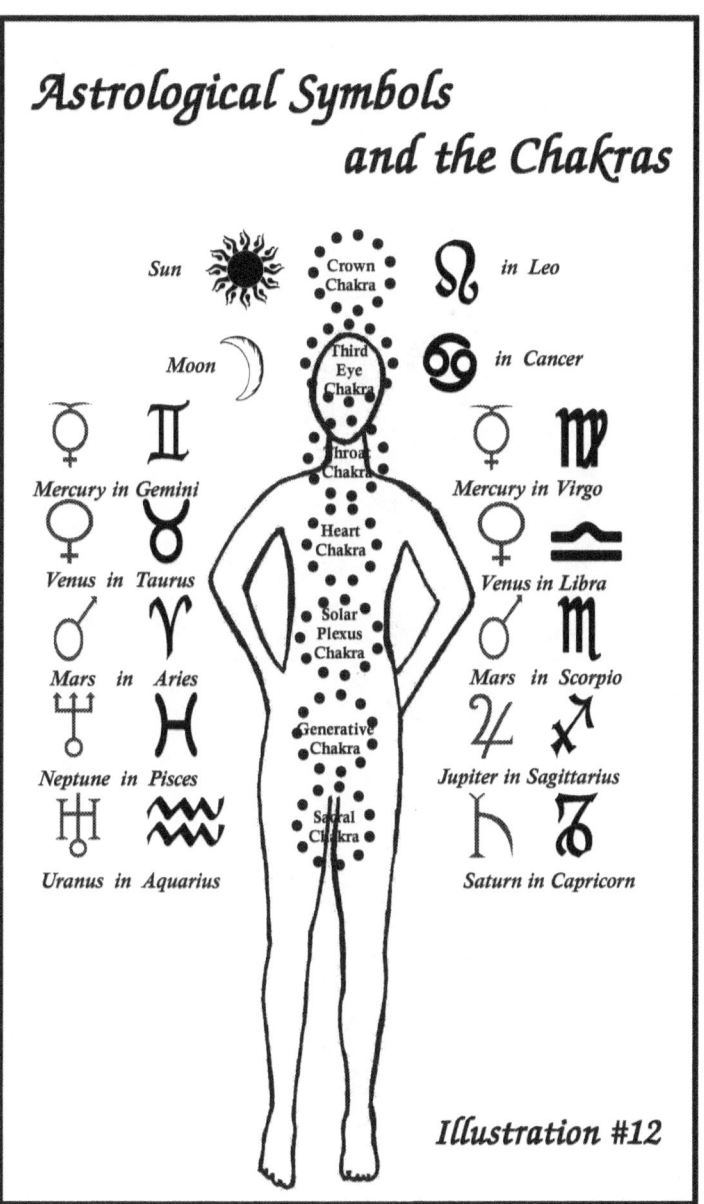

Illustration #12

Quick Guide to Practice Exercises

Thinking of and experiencing yourself & the world as energy 20-23

Becoming conscious of force and form .... 46 & 47

Learning to direct energy through the chakras
 Generative .... 59-60; 139-141 #2, 5, 6 &7;
 .... 202 #4
 Solar Plexus .... 94-95; 140 #3; 202 #3
 Heart ... 114 #1;116 #6; 140 #4; 141 #6; 202 #2
 Throat .... 160 #1; 161 #2; 201 #1
 Third Eye .... 182 #1, 2 &3

Learning to recognize chakra energies
 Generative .... 60 #s 2 & 3; & 139 #2
 Solar Plexus .... 95 #2; 96 #5; 140 #3
 Heart .... 115 #s 2 & 3; 116 #s4, 5, 6; 140 #4
 Throat 160-162
 Third Eye .... 182 #1 & 2

Learning the full breath and using it to direct energy:
 .... 139-141; 160 #1; 161 #2; 182 #s 1, 2, & 3

Observing self: .... 73-74; 115-117 #2, 3, 4, 5 & 8;
.... 142 & 143; 162 #6; 183 #s 5-7

"Cooking" a life experience: .... 95 #3

Identifying rapports: .... 96 #4

Gaining direction in your life: .... 117 #7

Cleansing the psyche: .... 142 #s 8 & 9; 224 #2

Using the voice to release power: ....
.... 161-162 #3, 4, 5; 201 #1

Building new faculties/skills:
    Meditation .... 182 #4
    Mental Telepathy .... 183 #s 7 & 8
    Faculties of Consciousness .... 224 #1
    Consciousness Skills .... 225 #3
    Changes of Form .... 225 #4

Bibliography

Books Referenced in the Text:

Bourgeault, Cynthia. *The Wisdom Way of Knowing: Reclaiming an Ancient Tradition to Awaken the Heart.* San Francisco: A Wiley Imprint, Jossey-Bass, 2003.

Bucke, Richard Maurice. *Cosmic Consciousness.* New York: Arkana Books, 1991.

Goldman, Jonathan. *Healing Sounds: The Power of Harmonics.* Rockport, MA: Element Books, 1995.

Keyes, Laurel Elizabeth. *Toning.* Marina del Rey, CA: DeVorss & Co., 1990.

Krishna, Gopi. *Kundalini: The Evolutionary Energy in Man.* Berkeley, CA: Shambala, 1971.

Lorrance, Arleen. *The Love Principles.* Scottsdale, AZ: Teleos Imprint, 2001.

_____. *The Love Project,* San Diego: LP Publications, 1972.

Paulus, Mariamne. *Awakening to Wisdom.* Scottsdale, AZ: Teleos Imprint, 2003.

———————— *Four Paths To Union.* Scottsdale, AZ: Teleos Imprint, 2001.

Pike, Diane Kennedy. *Life As A Waking Dream.* New York: Riverhead Books, 1997.

Pushkin, Alexander. *The Poems, Prose and Plays of Alexander Pushkin.* New York: Modern Library, 1943.

Vitvan. *The Basic Teachings of the School of the Natural Order*, Volumes 1, 2, & 3. Baker, NV: School of the Natural Order, 1971.

Books for Further Reading:

Bailey, Alice A. *Esoteric Astrology: A Treatise on the Seven Rays.* New York: Lucis Trust.

Bennett, John G. *Energies: Material, Vital, Cosmic.* Charles Town, WV: Claymont Communications, 1989.

Campbell, Don G. *The Roar of Silence: Healing Powers of Breath, Tone & Music.* Wheaton, IL: The Theosophical Publishing House, 1989.

Davies, Brenda. *The 7 Healing Chakras: Unlocking Your Body's Energy Centers.* Berkeley, CA: Ulysses Press, 2000.

Bibliography 245

Goldman, Jonathan. *Shifting Frequencies.* Flagstaff, AZ: Light Technology Publishing, 1998.

Hodson, Geoffrey. *The Seven Human Temperaments.* Wheaton, IL: The Theosophical Publishing House, 1981.

Judith, Anodea & Selene Vega. *The Sevenfold Journey.* Berkeley, CA: The Crossing Press, 1993.

Judith, Anodea. *Wheels of Life: A User's Guide to the Chakra System.* St. Paul, MN: Llewellyn Publications, 1992.

Karagulla, Shafica and Dora van Gelder Kunz. *The Chakras and the Human Energy Fields.* Wheaton, IL: The Theosophical Publishing House, 1989.

Myss, Caroline. *Anatomy of the Spirit: The Seven Stages of Power and Healing.* New York: Harmony Books, 1996.

Oken, Alan. *Soul-Centered Astrology: A Key to Your Expanding Self.* Freedom, CA: The Crossing Press, 1996.

Pert, Candace B. *Molecules of Emotion: The Science Behind Mind-Body Medicine.* New York: A Touchstone Book, Simon & Schuster, 1997.

Shealy, C. Norman & Myss, Caroline M. *The Creation of Health: The Emotional, Psychological, and Spiritual Responses that Promote Health and Healing.* Walpole, NH: Stillpoint Publishing, 1993.

Vitvan. *The Seven Rays of Development.* Baker, NV: School of the Natural Order.

Websites:

To learn more about Mariamne Paulus (Diane Kennedy Pike) and the work of Teleos Institute, go to www.teleosinstitute.com

To learn more about Vitvan (born Ralph De Bit), an American Master, go online to www.vitvan.org or write to the School of the Natural Order, PO Box 150, Baker, NV 89311.

www.ingramcontent.com/pod-product-compliance
Lightning Source LLC
Chambersburg PA
CBHW031239290426
44109CB00012B/360